Praise for Purpose

'I was moved to tears many times throughout this lightning-rod of a book... but the new, additional chapters just floored me! Jessica generously shares the rigour of her own transformation journey so we can all receive the pure, golden wisdom that is birthed through her. With unguarded emotion, poetry and passion, *Purpose* shows you how to answer your soul's deepest calling through healing yourself.'

SOPHIE BASHFORD, AUTHOR OF *YOU ARE A GODDESS*

'There are good books and there are great books. The great one's leave you a little changed, a little different. They even have the power to make you a better person. Jessica Huie's book did just that for me. It is a modern day hero's quest, a coming of age, a woman's search for meaning. It is beautiful and magical and painful to read. The stripped back honesty of Jessica's story allowed me a window into my own search for meaning.'

RACHEL PENDERED, FOUNDER OF MEDIA ZOO LTD

'Jessica's book is a timely call for us to enquire within to find our true purpose in our work and our life. With unflinching honesty, Jessica charts her own journey to her life's purpose in what is a hugely relatable read.'

THE SUNDAY TIMES

'Jessica's raw and honest style of writing about her struggles and spiritual journey is gripping, relatable and moving. With each chapter, she provides a thought-provoking message that helps you move forward on your own journey of self-discovery.'

VEX KING, AUTHOR OF *GOOD VIBES, GOOD LIFE* AND *HEALING IS THE NEW HIGH*

T0286219

'An inspirational story of one woman's journey of heartache and emotional pain as she confronts the death of her loving father and her ensuing grief, using it as a catalyst for self-discovery, spiritual awakening and remembering her soul's purpose. A compelling story, this book leaves the reader with hope as her sadness is transmuted into healing as she steps into a brighter future.'

ANITA MOORJANI, NEW YORK TIMES BESTSELLING AUTHOR OF *DYING TO BE ME* AND *WHAT IF THIS IS HEAVEN?*

'I love the book and I adore Jessica. I cried three times reading it! It's really brilliant and I completely resonated with her message.'

SUZY GREAVES, FORMER EDITOR-IN-CHIEF, *PSYCHOLOGIES*

'*Purpose* reads like an engaging novel. Within these pages are so many individual lessons. As readers, we can all see ourselves in Jessica Huie's experiences. We read them as our own, and in so doing, we get the meaning in the lesson. This book is ultimately a journey back to ourselves, and through finding ourselves, we find our true purpose.'

DAVID R. HAMILTON PHD, AUTHOR OF 9 BOOKS INCLUDING *THE FIVE SIDE EFFECTS OF KINDNESS*

'*Purpose* is a must read for anyone seeking something more from their life. Down-to-earth and inspiring, Jessica shows us how to follow the niggle and create the life we were born to live.'

REBECCA CAMPBELL, BESTSELLING AUTHOR OF *LIGHT IS THE NEW BLACK* AND *RISE SISTER RISE*

'An arresting memoir that will inspire anyone looking to smash through ceilings. Jessica's spirit, tenacity and heart leaps off the page.'

SOPHIE SCOTT, FOUNDER AND FORMER EDITOR-IN-CHIEF, *BALANCE* MAGAZINE

'Jessica Huie's journey to self and purpose is perfection. Heartwarming and honest.'

NIA LONG, ACTRESS

'Truthful and powerful. Jessica courageously opens up in a way which allows the reader to experience her enlightenment and reflect on their own in doing so. A must read for anyone seeking purpose in their life.'
FUSE ODG

'A beautiful, touching book and timely invitation to us all to free ourselves from the masks, and to speak and live our truth.'
ALI BASTIAN, ACTRESS

'Jessica's journey to finding purpose has been one of huge inspiration and joy. Once you read her story and understand her approach to life, you are left feeling refreshed, rebuilt and ready to take on the world.'
ESTELLE, GRAMMY AWARD-WINNING ARTIST

'In a rare and unparalleled voice of beauty and grace, Jessica Huie leads us to where true power rests; within. Jessica demonstrates the unique and life-changing courage it takes to listen and also to act on our soul's desire. There's no greater inspiration than the imperative her story offers us; our purpose is to live in alignment with love.'
MEGGAN WATTERSON, AUTHOR OF *MARY MAGDALENE REVEALED*

P U R P O S E

PURPOSE

Find Your Truth

and Embrace

Your Calling

JESSICA HUIE

HAY HOUSE

Carlsbad, California • New York City
London • Sydney • New Delhi

Published in the United Kingdom by:
Hay House UK Ltd, The Sixth Floor, Watson House, 54 Baker Street, London
W1U 7BU
Tel: +44 (0)20 3927 7290; Fax: +44 (0)20 3927 7291; www.hayhouse.co.uk

Published in the United States of America by:
Hay House Inc., PO Box 5100, Carlsbad, CA 92018-5100
Tel: (1) 760 431 7695 or (800) 654 5126; Fax: (1) 760 431 6948 or (800) 650 5115
www.hayhouse.com

Published in Australia by:
Hay House Australia Ltd, 18/36 Ralph St, Alexandria NSW 2015
Tel: (61) 2 9669 4299; Fax: (61) 2 9669 4144; www.hayhouse.com.au

Published in India by:
Hay House Publishers India, Muskaan Complex, Plot No.3, B-2,
Vasant Kunj, New Delhi 110 070
Tel: (91) 11 4176 1620; Fax: (91) 11 4176 1630; www.hayhouse.co.in

Text © Jessica Huie, 2018, 2021

The moral rights of the author have been asserted.

All rights reserved. No part of this book may be reproduced by any mechanical,
photographic or electronic process, or in the form of a phonographic recording;
nor may it be stored in a retrieval system, transmitted or otherwise be copied
for public or private use, other than for 'fair use' as brief quotations embodied
in articles and reviews, without prior written permission of the publisher.

The information given in this book should not be treated as a substitute for
professional medical advice; always consult a medical practitioner. Any
use of information in this book is at the reader's discretion and risk. Neither
the author nor the publisher can be held responsible for any loss, claim
or damage arising out of the use, or misuse, of the suggestions made, the
failure to take medical advice or for any material on third-party websites.

A catalogue record for this book is available from the British Library.

Tradepaper ISBN: 978-1-4019-6522-8
E-book ISBN: 978-1-78817-808-2
Audiobook ISBN: 978-1-78817-667-5

10 9 8 7 6 5 4 3 2 1

Interior images: Danita Delimont/Shutterstock

Printed in the United States of America

This book is dedicated to my children, my family – genetic and those gifted along my path.

All of my Purpose Academy and Purpose retreat fam for the love, learning and connection.

The Hay House team for being so much more than simply the publishers of my book.

Nana, you are a blessing in my life, my sister.

To Lisa Lawrence for holding space for my silence when I had no words.

To Sophie Bashford for just being alive at this moment in time and my sister for the ride.

To the hummingbirds, who've taught me how to fly free.

To Lion.

And to DKG, my beautiful surprise.

I love you.

X

Contents

Introduction

*'Some of us on this Earth are the candles
and lanterns, flickering lights reassuringly
pointing out the way in the bends within
this vast tunnel, which is life on Earth.'*

ERNEST LIVINGSTONE HUIE (MY DAD)

This isn't the book I was supposed to write. I built a successful 20-year career in media, first as a showbiz journalist before shifting into public relations, launching a card company that made history as the UK's first multicultural card brand stocked in chain stores. So a book on personal branding or starting a business would've been far more conventional and perhaps professionally strategic. But then I've never been one for convention and as life would have it, this book chose me.

I've spent almost two decades challenging perceptions – both of myself and others. Crusading for equality, representation and inclusion across multiple sectors, my own background as a girl from a council estate who became a mother at 17 became the kick-ass engine behind my desire to close society's opportunity gaps. Whilst I've been fortunate to have had many accolades and awards bestowed upon me for my outward accomplishments, it's my internal journey that's been the most profound, presenting the steepest learning curves.

Sometimes, as we continue down well-trodden paths, we find ourselves presented with the option to detour. A chance to explore an alluring alternate road not configured on our sat nav. For me, this book is that path and the mere process of writing it has been laden with the gift of memories bubbling up to the surface of my consciousness, sometimes making for some uncomfortable learning.

The idea of writing a book first occurred to me several years ago. As a publicist I recognized that triumph over tribulation, paired with history-making in the high street and celebrity jaunts, had the ingredients of a good read. But how to weave together the different facets of my life and work them into one book? By Christmas 2015, I was tired. The 18 years spent striving, struggling and battling all the time had taken their toll. This controlled forwards motion had certainly paid dividends, taking me all over the globe, introducing me to many people and different worlds, transforming my life. And it had been incredible. But after eight years running my businesses I'd become stale and spent. The passion was gone and rolling out of bed at 5:30 a.m. to plan my day no longer filled me with enthusiasm. I needed a fresh new challenge, to learn again, to feel awe.

The first phase of my adult life had been spent building and accruing experience as a journalist and PR consultant, as much of it as possible, in order to build a life for my daughter and me. I'd spent it building my network, exposing myself to different facets of the media industry and having a blast in the process. Phase two was all about entrepreneurship. The thrill of taking the embryo of an idea, born out of a desire to do things differently and to contribute, through to concept and implementation. Having built and maintained what I'd birthed, I earned notoriety along the way. But for the first time since I was 18, without a goal, life felt uncertain again. I couldn't continue as things were. My soul was unfulfilled and I began to feel inauthentic, merely delivering because I had outgoings to cover, but the zest for the job had dissipated.

Then my dad fell ill. The period of caring for him brought us closer than ever and for the first time in my life, I experienced first-hand what it is to be truly selfless. If parenthood was level one in the lesson of giving, caring for a love of your life when they're dying is the advanced course. Knowing the clock is ticking in your time left together and breathing in every word. Living for each conversation lest it might be the last, while losing inhibition and barriers as the old distinctions of your roles become irrelevant in place of the new demands of their disease, altered life as I knew it forever.

In those weeks and days between life and death, time froze. Everything outside of my interaction and anything I could do from moment to moment to ease Dad's physical suffering or quieten his mind were all-encompassing. I existed for him only and found a joy in doing so, which brought a momentary happiness as pure as the day I heard my baby, Monet, laugh for the first time.

The last words my dad ever said to me were 'Hold my hand.' So I did and after four days of waiting, dreading yet anticipating the end, he died, my hand in his, his in mine. In the outside world Britain was exiting Europe. In my world I was exiting life as I knew it.

Grief wrenched me out of the day-to-day running of the business. It sent me silently crashing to my knees and broke me open, forcing me to surrender. It was as though the noise of constant activity that had pervaded my life from the moment I made the decision aged 18 to transform it, ceased. The din subsided and was replaced with stillness. Along with the relentless ache of loss in my chest was an unexpected peace. And then the magic happened.

I began to notice things that had always been there with new eyes. Each morning I'd experience the sun rising and the notice the formation of the clouds as though I were seeing it for the very first time. I started to feel things in a new way, too. I became connected to life in all its forms, in the most powerful, inexplicable way. I was in the moment, awake, and though I longed for my father's presence, I felt his spirit in and around me in everything I did. It was incredible. Within this quiet, with my oars now entirely still, the waves parted, and complete and utter clarity lay before me. My dad had been such a mammoth part of my identity that when he passed on, I was hurtled into my ground zero and forced to redefine my place in the world. I went from being raw and lost without him, to finding me *because* of him.

The calling for something new, that new purpose that would fill me with passion and give me reason and possibilities, opening doors to a new life once again, was right there. After desperately searching for signs about what to do with the next phase of my life, heartbreak over my dad's death forced me to stop searching for my next calling. The panic I felt about the uncertainty was a new state of being for someone who was usually ambitious and focused. But when I stopped, the answers found me. I had begun writing as a cathartic coping mechanism when Dad's illness took over and his words of wisdom could be heard no more, following which my pen became powerful. What began as an outpouring of despair evolved into the project of my tomorrow. This very book. A parting kiss goodbye from him, through me.

For my entire life, I've required a level of controlled perfection of myself that has been impossible to realize and sustain. I've cracked a silent whip on my back with a ferociousness no enemy would inflict upon me, demanding more, better, to the detriment of my self-worth, as 'enough' became an unobtainable mirage. Not unusual behaviour for those of us who figured early on in life that control was a method of personal safeguarding. I've been addicted to controlling every aspect of my life, and wherever possible the people in it, for as long as I can remember. There's a certain feeling of comfort and security in forcing outcomes before they can occur naturally. In cushioning blows, both mine and of those I love, by leaping in front of risks and potential problems before they happen. Working all the hours God sent at the sacrifice of sleep to safeguard me from not being successful (even when

I'd become successful). Micromanaging others in case they didn't do things to the standard I would do them. Sabotaging relationships in case they didn't work out. And then exhaling like a weird psychopath, relaxing into an overworked, lonely but familiarly comforting depression, almost like 'Phew! That was close – I almost lost control and became happy.'

I used to cushion my daughter's every move without even realizing it. In an effort to avoid her ever having to feel disappointment, pain or discomfort, I was always several steps ahead of her, sussing out the terrain for my little princess. And then one day when I realized she was already a teenager, I began to notice that I'd ask her to do a simple task and she'd give up halfway through before asking for my assistance. Not because she was lazy, but because I'd set the tone for her disempowerment. Realizing that this wasn't the kind of parent I wanted to be, I began to take action to change that lifelong habit.

Giving up my addiction to controlling events in my *own* life, however, took a lot longer to spot and even longer to rectify. I'm still not reformed – it's going to be a lifelong practice of unlearning the counterproductive habit of thinking that I can force things into turning out exactly the way I want, just by applying more pressure, more force and by controlling situations. I'm not alone in this addiction. I believe that many of us are in the same backward-rowing boat, paddling desperately against the force of a high tide, determined to make it to the shore. And not just make it to the shore, but to continue through the throttling waves. Meanwhile, the seagulls chuckle at us from the sky. With their bird's-eye view, they can see that if we would only pause for a moment, the seas would calm and the current would carry us to a paradise on the horizon.

I'd always believed that achieving anything in life was entirely down to me. I was responsible for my own life and its outcomes, everything resting on my weary shoulders. I believed in God or a universal force, but as a sort of abstract concept that had everything to do with being a good person and nothing to do with how my life turned out from a practical standpoint. All that changed when Dad passed away.

I experienced first-hand that there is so much more to our experience on this Earth than we think. We've been taught that taking action and working hard is the key to success, and certainly taking action is necessary. But if we have faith and consider, as I do today, the fact that we're being completely supported by a force beyond our worldly comprehension, then we'll open ourselves up to an incredible power, enabling more possibilities to what we might become. It is this force that's just waiting for us to take our foot off the gas, so it can guide and carry us to our purpose on this Earth. We're not victims of life who are simply reacting to events that occur. On the contrary, we can and do influence our own reality. The journey of discovering how we can tap into this source power, unleashing it to transform and co-create our reality, continues to be a beautifully enlightening and enchanted adventure – and believe me, I've had a few…

Caring for my dad taught me the truth about who I am, giving me the final parting gift of wisdom and insight into my life's purpose, after a year that changed my life. I believe that the best gifts should be shared, and this is mine.

⌒

The Backstory

'I had no idea that being your authentic self could make me as rich as I've become. If I had, I'd have done it a lot earlier.'
OPRAH WINFREY

Stepping up and out requires gumption. I was 19 when I walked into the Bond Street offices of the man who at that time was Britain's most powerful publicist, and I was going to make my mark. The exercise spent sitting cross-legged on the living-room floor, highlighter in hand, crossing off the names of public relations agencies listed in the *Yellow Pages*, proved successful. A telephone call and an interview later, and I'd landed a two-week work experience placement at what was then London's most powerful PR agency. Failure wasn't an option, as it was just months since my reality had been benefits and hopelessness.

I was still living on the 15th floor of a council tower block amongst many other teen mums and suddenly I found myself in a lift with Simon Cowell. I'd passed 15 paparazzi outside the front entrance all waiting to see Rebecca Loos (of David

Beckham 'fame') walk in to meet with my then boss. She was to share details of what went on to become the country's highest paid kiss-and-tell story ever. I was millions of miles from the shore of my comfort zone in this glossy, glamorous office amongst privately educated Surrey girls, with whom I shared little in common. While my stomach was in knots with nerves, I was exhilarated. I was about to take the first step in building a life for my two-year-old daughter and myself, and for the first time in many months I felt alive.

I'd become a mum at the age of 17, intentionally. Somewhere in my childhood my self-esteem had become eroded and by the time I was 17, I figured that starting a family would give me purpose. My parents' wish was for me to become the first in our family to go to university. The problem was, I didn't know anybody who looked like me or who lived where I lived (a council estate in Westbourne Park) who'd done that. My perception of all universities was of an old-school Oxbridge institution in which I wouldn't fit or belong, so I rebelled and took the matter of what to do with my life into my own naive, ill-experienced hands. I couldn't even boil a pot of pasta when Monet was born. Emotionally immature and practically inept, the reality of my experience, far from *The Cosby Show* family life I'd envisioned, was a rude awakening.

My parents had their challenges, and my two brothers and I certainly suffered from the impact of being in a household that at times was entirely dysfunctional. But we were loved – incredibly loved – and I learned as I grew older just how much of a struggle my parents had encountered in their own journeys. The mere fact they'd stayed together to raise us was nothing short of miraculous, testament to two people who wanted the world for their children. Although Mum and Dad had worked seven days a week to give us a diary of extracurricular activities to rival the most middle class of families, when we looked outside our window it was bleak. At that time prostitutes frequented Westbourne Park Road and were constantly moved on by police officers attempting to mask the deprivation that lay beneath what was becoming the new yuppie Notting Hill of London. The crack cocaine epidemic devastated the community and even our strict upbringing, which meant we were forbidden to play out on the estate, couldn't shelter us from seeing the gaunt figures on street corners searching for their next high.

Teenage boys took to the stairwells of our estate smoking cannabis, disconnected from the outside world, numbing themselves to the bleakness of their realities. And we became passive smokers to their hopelessness as we passed them on our journey home from school. Teenage pregnancy was at its height just at the time I was moving into puberty, wrestling with the cloud of my immediate environment, balanced against parents with big dreams for their offspring. It wasn't all hopelessness. There was a strong sense of community in our local area, and on summer days Bessie the 'sky-juice' lady would sell her ice and syrup drinks to us kids by the basketball court. I'd sometimes interrupt my errand to the shop to meander down to Portobello Market, which was the vibrant backdrop to our neighbourhood.

Still, the instability in my family home left me an introspective teenager. I was desperate for a stable home, and so at 17 I decided to opt out of life as it was, take matters into my own hands and start my own family. I'd create a purpose for my life – I'd become a mum.

I'll never forget the tears in my father's eyes when I told him I was pregnant. He was devastated. Dad had arrived in England on a boat from St Elizabeth, Jamaica, when he was 20 years old in 1953. Clad in a sharp three-piece suit with polished boots and qualified to teach, he didn't know a soul in a land that received him with hostility. Shipped away by his mother to break up a relationship with a woman my strict Jamaican grandparents felt was inappropriate, he was quickly forced into earning a living.

His career began as Nottingham's first black bus driver (his Jamaican qualifications weren't recognized in England) before an altercation with a passenger who called him 'Sambo' landed him in prison – a story worthy of a book in its own right. My father endured poverty, racism, loneliness and tragedy during his 84 years, but my birth in 1980 was a turning point that saw him hang up his colourful existence and spend 25 years driving a minicab in London's Kensal Rise to raise our family. A committed father, he was a wise and philosophical man, who used to cut up oranges to teach us fractions and who accompanied us to every possible park in London each Sunday.

It broke his heart when I fell pregnant, so much so that he couldn't bring himself to speak to me. Soon afterwards, I was given a room in a hostel in King's Cross, London. A place where I awoke one night, alone and heavily pregnant, to find an army of cockroaches parading across the wall above my head. Those were difficult days. My daughter's dad was around at the time, but he was as immature and ill-equipped for parenthood as I was.

I recall feeling as though I were existing beneath the surface of life, sort of alive but not actually part of the hive of activity of commuters boarding tubes to varying destinations. The front cover of the *Daily Mail* seemed to shout weekly about the scourge of teen mums getting pregnant to sponge off the state and secure council flats. People didn't smile at you as a pregnant teen. At that time they tutted, shaking their heads in open disdain at the sight of a child with child, wearing a tracksuit and wandering aimlessly in what was one of London's most deprived areas in the late nineties.

The little self-worth I had dissipated, and I became deeply depressed and frightened. It wasn't a clinical depression – at least it went undiagnosed – but more to do with the pressing issue of needing a home to which I could return with my baby once she arrived. Just how I would manage in this new existence I'd blindly chosen took priority above my mental health. I didn't once consider that the fog that enveloped me from the moment I opened my eyes, with the occasional dark thought of whether stepping off the underground platform into nonexistence would bring peace, was anything other than simply the consequence of my choices.

My family and friends and society as a whole seemed to write me off, and their prognosis became mine. What on earth was going to become of my baby and me? I had four GCSEs, having been expelled from school for stealing trainers for a boy from my brothers' school while on work experience, and no knowledge of how to change a nappy, let alone raise a child.

The looks and comments from strangers began to affect me, to the extent that I'd avoid the walk to the post office to collect my income support. Queuing outside for a state handout was the antithesis of the pride my hard-working parents had instilled in me. I began to hibernate inside without money or food until hunger forced me to submit and do the walk of shame in order to buy bread, milk and cheese.

There are moments in all of our lives when opportunities present themselves and, if we seize them, a door slides open to a new set of opportunities which we couldn't possibly have had the foresight or imagination to predict. The trouble is, these moments never have the word 'opportunity' stamped on them when they arrive.

My first life-changing opportunity showed up in the form of a health visitor. The typical kind who came to my flat to check how baby Monet and I were getting on. My parents had been clear that I was to handle my own responsibilities and I'm so grateful now that they took that stance; though at the time I thought I would die from exhaustion.

I shared with the health visitor the fact that I spent much of my day in tears, which made it difficult to function. That admission was about me acknowledging that I was *not* OK with either my life or myself at that point. But it was that same honesty that created the opportunity for the health visitor to suggest that I return to college and complete my A-levels. I felt I'd been handed an olive branch, a second chance, for she gave me permission to dust off early dreams and pursue them. Common sense, one would think, but far from it. It was revelatory, as nobody had suggested that a return to education was even a possibility at that point. My admission was the catalyst to her opening a door, a door that became the first of many to be opened by other individuals, who consistently showed up on my journey offering yet more opportunities, support and lessons – but taking action always came first.

Just three months later I was back at the very college I'd dropped out of, much to the bemusement of some of the tutors who'd taught me pre-baby. But this time I was a different teenager. Gone was the arrogant attitude of someone who had better places to be and instead I carried my books under my arm with pride. I remember distinctly the feeling that having a destination gave me. The moments under my duvet where I'd wished the world would swallow me and my bump up were behind me. A small glimmer of hope in the form of re-education had reawakened my aspirations, and while I was very much at the start of a very long and tough road to building a life, I was taking the first steps towards it.

Tutors suggested I should stick to one A-level, given I was only taking evening classes in order to care for my baby during the day. But having booked on a fast-track, intensive one-year A-level course, I needed two A-levels in 12 months in order to secure a place at university. Every cell in my body desperately needed to secure that place. I couldn't wait. I was going to be a journalist, I decided, as I'd always loved writing as a child and so I could interview celebrities. Possibility had sparked an interest in me and while it was impossible not to feel the distance between that dream and my reality, that dream was my sanity. Especially during the early hours of the morning when my baby and I cried, when I was desperate to have the space to complete my coursework, often beating myself up for what I considered to be a lack of maternal capability.

I lived for my twice-weekly evening college classes, simultaneously falling head over heels in love with my daughter, while experiencing in abundance the love and sense of purpose I'd been so desperate for. She was beautiful and in the way that babies pick up on our energy so deftly, she cared for me as much as I did for her. We became a team early on and I promised myself in those beautifully tough days when we had nothing that I'd create a life for us that was far from mediocre. I had no clear plan, only a vague end goal, which involved a great education for her, and travel and showbiz writing for me. I've no doubt now that the fire and intention behind that desire has everything to do with the events that followed.

And so the first day of the rest of my life found me in a lift with Simon Cowell. I'd gained an A and a C grade in A-level sociology and English literature respectively, securing me a place at Middlesex University, on the acclaimed National Council for the Training of Journalists (NCTJ) course. Piers Morgan studied there and while I saw a framed picture of this middle-aged man on the classroom wall, it meant nothing to me at the time. Later I met him as Editor of the *Sunday Mirror*, and worked closely with his office staff before he left for Hollywood and a career as a chat show host.

'You're cute. Can you sing?' said Simon.

I went on to relive this scenario in my mind over and over for many months. In my mind's eye, I burst into Mariah Carey's 'Hero', while Simon's jaw dropped in awe, his eyes glazing over at the prospect of turning me into his label's latest star. In reality, I blushed at being spoken to by someone who was not only important, but also famous, and mumbled that I could 'hold a note'. Then I shuffled out into the office, where I'd arrived for the first day of my internship.

Looking around at the bevy of chic, cool media women behind desks, it was a different universe. Even the walk from the number 7 bus stop down Bond Street had been life-changing. *I work on Bond Street!* I thought, hearing the magnificence of that statement again and again in my head.

That first day was epic. After meeting the team and 'office Mummy' Dee, who'd first interviewed me for the role, I was invited to the press launch of the TV show *Pop Idol*, which preceded *X Factor*. That afternoon was surreal. I found myself as a passenger in Simon's souped-up sports car, whizzing through the streets of the West End to be part of the crew on what became one of TV's most successful talent shows. I hardly spoke. I was drunk on this new world of lights and cameras, wealth and celebrity. I was 19, and just a year earlier life seemed to have plunged to its ultimate low in a King's

Cross hostel frequented by prostitutes and drug addicts, and yet here I was!

At the end of a dizzying afternoon, I was offered a lift home by Simon Cowell's driver. I remember hoping desperately that somebody, anybody, would see me being dropped off in this chauffeur-driven car with Britain's most famous TV superstar in the front passenger seat. Sod's law it was a quiet evening on the estate that night, and from one Bond Street lift to another in the Brunel Estate, I was transported back up to the 15th floor, where my two-year-old baby girl was waiting with my mother for my return.

I floated through those next few days. Life seemed to have developed a Destiny's Child 'Independent Women' soundtrack. I was off benefits and never had to face the soul-destroying staff at the housing benefit office again. I had a weekend job in Russell & Bromley and with a mean hand at upselling handbags with matching shoes, combined with my student loan, my baby and I might have been far from flush, but I was able to hold my head high.

When I passed my driving test, my dad bought me a white Nissan Micra, which I posed in, windows open with Beyoncé, Michelle and Kelly blasting out 'Independent Women'. With life's sweet irony, five years later a seven-year-old Monet strolled beside me into one of the most opulent suites of The May Fair Hotel, London to interview Kelly Rowland (to whom I'd become UK publicist) for her school project. A product of a big dream and with a burning ambition herself, Kelly was happy to carve out time from recording with David Guetta between our packed itinerary of journalist interviews in order to be the subject of Monet's 'inspiring person' homework. Considering she was in one of the most successful girl groups (selling 68 million records worldwide), it's heartwarming to know she still made time for my daughter.

At home I was a mummy and a uni student, and at the PR office I was a media guru in the making (at least in my own mind). I was unstoppable, indomitable and talented. I kept the fact I was a mother secret from the office staff, not wanting to risk quashing their perception of this ambitious young uni student.

It couldn't have been more than three or four days after starting that the phone rang at home and Monet answered a squeaky 'Hello'. I leaped across the room for the handset. Grabbing it from Monet, my heart sank as I heard Dee's voice on the other end of the line sounding somewhat amused.

'Is that your sister, Jessica?' she asked.

I hesitated. 'No, it's my daughter.'

What felt like an hour of silence followed. By the time I hung up, I felt like the biggest imposter on the planet. My cover was blown and I'd been exposed for what I was – not a young future star of British media, but a former state-scrounging, crappy teenage mum who didn't belong on Bond Street, let alone in Simon Cowell's car. I'd blown it. The dream was over. I was a fraud.

My confidence and mood plummeted for a few days as I retreated, allowing the niggling internal voice back into my life, the one that mocked my dream of a bigger life that I'd begun to craft. That's the problem with having your validity and sense of self wrapped up in anything as external as another person's perception. It's why pop stars and sports legends crumble when their careers and stardom wane. And it's why the current generation of teenagers, raised in a society in which social media 'likes' dictate self-esteem, are plagued with anxiety. Sourcing our self-esteem from anything other than the essence of our character has a sell-by date; though I didn't know this then, of course – I just thought I was a loser.

I toyed with the idea of not going back the following week. The thought of walking back into the office without my mask, as the person I really was, terrified me. But the following week the call I'd been dreading, in which I was asked not to return, never came, so I found the strength to return. It was a different walk I took down Bond Street this time. Everything felt a little less dreamlike and more real.

I'll never forget the warmth with which I was greeted. Or the card from my boss that was handed to me at the end of the day, in which the message read: 'You are a credit to yourself and to your parents. Welcome to the family.' Along with the cheque for £5,000 (cue Destiny's Child soundtrack again). It was more money than I'd ever seen in one go. It was mind-blowing.

My office mum, Dee, later explained that they'd all been blown away by the fact I was juggling the internship with a degree, a weekend job and raising my baby, and it had endeared me to them. It was my first lesson in the power of being who you are. They liked the real me more than the pretend version. And

I'm forever grateful for that lesson; though it would take many years for the simple logic in the power of authenticity to truly sink in.

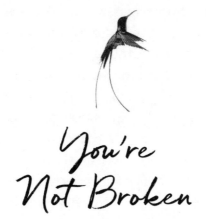

You're Not Broken

'Until you heal the wounds of your past, you will continue to bleed.'
IYANLA VANZANT

What's your story? What's the default setting that rumbles beneath every interaction you have in both your personal and professional life? The chances are you've never stopped to consider it or maybe you're conscious enough to have observed it, but haven't yet found the tools to reframe the internal script that we all have running within us. Consider for a moment your internal dialogue when things go wrong. Often, it's a tale of woe about not being smart enough, slim enough, courageous enough – generally about not being enough – but go deeper and reflect on the life story you've written about your journey so far and explore what you find.

Mine was that I was a former teen mum with a dysfunctional childhood who'd spent her life struggling to overcome challenge but had survived. If it were an image, it would've been of a woman battling against tornado-force winds, being blasted from left to right, striving to stay upright against the force of the sheer pressure of the elements. Of somehow arriving at a destination, battered and bruised, not to mention windswept – before the hurricane began to rise again. Over and over again. There might have been a certain comforting triumph to my story, summoning notions of courage, resilience and strength, giving me the satisfaction of feeling I was a woman who persisted, the heroine in my self-penned story. But the reality was that my story was in fact completely disempowering, indeed a tool for keeping my life in a downhill spiral of struggle with momentary wins. It was a revelation when I finally realized this. The discovery that my tale – which I'd honed over the years to perfection, repeating and sharing it with others when asked about my background or success until it was the perfect script – was a fallacy. It was like curtains that had been closed for a lifetime were finally drawn back to reveal the light for the first time!

I'd truly believed for all of my adult life that I'd been affected by my early experiences, to the degree that these 'issues' became a part of who I was. It was intrinsic to the very fibre of my being, somehow stitched into my cells and hidden from the public at all costs – not good for my image. But it was a lie. Without realizing it, we brainwash ourselves through repetition, with stories about our suffering and trauma, crippling us into stagnation, holding us back from enjoying the full potential for our heart's desires. This is what we do. Every. Single. One. Of. Us. And the result? The universe responds accordingly, giving us exactly what we've manifested using our powerful unconscious focus on disempowering stories.

Only these stories we create have everything to do with our past and how we perceive it, and nothing to do with the lives we actually want to create.

That revelation, that incredible realization that our stories are merely a way of perceiving a series of events that keep us shackled to the past, changed both my outlook and my life. If you consider for just a moment that you have the power to choose a *new* way of perceiving everything that's ever happened to you and who you are as a result, it'll change your life forever.

Best of all, the resentment, pain, heartbreak and regret that we carry around unconsciously in our hearts, minds and bodies – making us ill and victims of our circumstances without even realizing it – will melt away, to be replaced by peace and unbridled power. A beautiful embryonic space from which you'll be free to harness the power to co-create, grow and design your life.

This point for consideration is one of the most important in this book. Create the space to consider it, to ponder on it. What's your story? You'll need to be brave and uncompromisingly honest with yourself to explore this question, as it requires you to unpick all of the threads sewn into the tapestry of your false identities over decades.

⌒

I was still shackled by my own outdated story of who I was 10 years after my Bond Street internship had evolved into me starting and building my own PR agency. My roster boasted clients like Samuel L. Jackson's Shooting Stars in Desert Nights annual charity event, business guru Hilary Devey of *Dragons' Den* and Destiny's Child star Kelly Rowland. I was featuring in the press on a regular basis for my achievements and wasn't yet 30 – not bad going for a girl who'd been existing on the underbelly of society some 10 years earlier. And yet my pain was not all champagne.

I recall a moment in 2009 in an infinity pool, where the water appears to merge with the skyline and ocean, in a spectacular villa in Turks and Caicos belonging to the then prime minister. I was part of a small group of celebrities and 'influencers' invited out to experience this paradise of islands. I was with my boyfriend at the time and daughter who was 11, and it was fabulousness personified. Swim-up bar served by waiters, DJs playing music, tanned limbs and drinks flowing against the backdrop of some of the most idyllic beaches in the world.

On the outside my life appeared to have been a pretty straightforward ascent, as I rose from one coveted position to another, with the media celebrating me as an 'inspirational woman' along the way. From the moment I walked back through my college doors as a new mum aged 18, I began to build a résumé of work, which continually brought yet more success and experience. To this day, I receive emails and messages from women in particular, explaining how they've 'followed my career' from columnist and high-profile PR to entrepreneur and change-maker. What wasn't public knowledge, that was far less admirable and sexy, were the internal battles I was fighting throughout.

There were fairly regular periods when I became overwhelmed by the sheer magnitude of my responsibilities. Times when I'd take on more and more, unable to say no, lest I fell back into the dark hole from which I'd crawled. Then there were the sporadic anxiety attacks, the crippling insecurity... And no matter how much I achieved, it was never enough. I beat myself up with ridiculous self-induced feats to achieve even more ridiculous levels of perfection. Worse, I sabotaged relationships I didn't belong in, all whilst desperately longing to create a solid family unit for my daughter and myself.

My problems weren't new. Their roots stemmed from my childhood, young adulthood experiences and the disempowering stories I'd told myself about who I was as a result. None of it was new. I'd just never given myself a spare moment to address what lay beneath the surface. Ambition was a plaster. Work was my drug and I was a functioning addict.

Like so many of us, I poured myself into accruing yet more work experience and internships, then mentors and up-skilling, in pursuit of success. I was a single mum on a mission and there was no way I was going to leave any opportunity untapped, not for my daughter, not for me. Achieving became an obsession, and I literally worked day and night, so much so that as soon as my daughter was asleep, I'd be back on my computer, working through the night on whatever project it was that we were working on at the time. To get ahead, to advance, anything that stopped me from having to pause and sit with myself. It paid dividends as action does. But the problem with success based on the terms that society has told us matter is that it doesn't cure the feeling of somehow not being enough. Of being an imposter on the verge of being found out, of questioning our abilities, of fear about what might happen should it all dissipate. And so while on the surface it might have appeared like I was living it up, backstage I was a wreck.

Aged 17, just a year prior to becoming a mother, I swallowed a pack of paracetamol then called an ambulance explaining that I knew somebody who wanted to die. It was a half-baked cry for help from a teenager who'd fallen out of the system and was desperately lacking in self-worth, rather than a real suicide attempt. I sort of knew that paracetamol alone wouldn't kill me, but I was fragile and low enough to test my theory. Sure enough, I went to sleep, much deeper than usual, but woke again the next day, not only to the same reality, but also with the feeling of a rain cloud over my pillow. Motherhood and worldly success gave me purpose and external validation, but it didn't heal the pain of my fragile inner child.

My early battles were those of a fear of being alone, a fear of raising a child, a fear of being a bad mother, a fear of never being successful enough, a fear of not fitting in, a fear of never having a traditional family unit, a fear of loneliness, a fear of heartache... a fear of everything. On the surface, however, I was fierce, confident and unstoppable. Putting on a brave face and persisting was part of my story, after all.

By my twenties I'd had enough and I embarked on a mission to 'fix' me with the same vigour I applied to my professional life. Thousands of pounds were spent on therapy talking through childhood traumas, attending ACA meetings for children of addicts, having reiki and engaging in life coaching. Then one day, after I'd trampled through another failed relationship, I sat in bed Googling for a panacea. I've no idea what I typed in the search bar to bring up meditation, but on that particular afternoon I was divinely guided to a website referring me to a centre in Covent Garden called Inner Space – a place where I was to be introduced to a new world.

Many of us hit our rock-bottom before we're jolted into the awareness of this alternate path, which has always been there for us to embark upon, but in my case had remained undiscovered. It might be after the painful ending of a relationship or a marriage, or following illness, a nervous breakdown, burnout, depression, grief... All these incidents that society perceives as rock-bottom are in fact the perfect vessels for transformation and our evolution from a life driven by fear. It can lead us from an underlying sense of lack to one of truth, where every moment is exactly as it should be.

For two decades, I felt my spirituality brush gently past my shoulders for fleeting moments – this sense of connectedness to something beyond the physical matter of life. Had I allowed myself even a moment's reflection, then being in the moment would have forced me to confront the reality that my remaining busy and occupied, continually 'doing', was merely masking the pain that remained beneath my accomplished surface. Being still and in the moment would have brought me face to face with my truth. For this silence would have meant listening to what the universe was telling me, when I didn't want to hear what needed to be heard. By continually 'doing' I was able to plaster over the whispers of wisdom within me. You've probably felt this connectedness in moments when you've stepped outside of your daily life. Moments when the beauty of the sea or the stars in the sky simply bowls you over. When the noise of the world and its seeming importance falls away, to be replaced, just for a moment, by a feeling of lush insignificance. Because far from being the centre of your universe, you are merely a particle in something more magnificent than your thinking mind can comprehend.

The old expression that says that only once we're ready to receive information or insight are we presented with it is certainly apt for me. It's now 10 years since the day I began my journey to discovering what was to change my entire perception of my life and ultimately myself. *We're not broken and there's nothing to fix.*

After a short course in learning to meditate at Inner Space, I began to understand that there was an alternate true reality, a sort of secret garden that existed within me. A quiet space that I could access by closing my eyes, concentrating on my breath and turning my focus within. It didn't come easily at first. Mine was the busiest of minds with umpteen thoughts, ideas and concerns whizzing across each other simultaneously. And my mind would wander to them habitually before I'd visualize myself turning from them and returning to the quiet movement of my breath, wafting back and forth like ocean waves against the shore. This was my initiation into spirituality and a connectedness with my true self. Not self-defined by awards, media adulation, boyfriends or expensive shoes, but by the true essence of me. During those moments when the outside world became crazy, I'd wander into my private space where only the present moment existed and through closed eyes I'd seek solace in the peace. Discovering meditation was like the ultimate exhale, unearthing a door to blissful quiet.

It wasn't something I nailed overnight. On many occasions, I found it near impossible to still my mind at all and I'd float off with each thought like a wild dog straining on a leash, leading me away from the focus on my breath. But with practice, I slowly retrained my mind to centre for a period of time. I found guided meditations hugely helpful during this process, and still find them a useful way to rein in my focus to the now and pin it on listening to the voice on the audio. Then one day, after practising somewhat inconsistently over a period of a few months, I found I melted into the most delicious quiet space inside myself. A space in which there was nothing else but that present, perfect moment. No painful past, no fearful future, just the pure heaven of silence in that moment. On opening my eyes reluctantly, I felt centred and suddenly more able to cope with whatever presented itself in my day – and I understood what all the fuss was about.

There isn't any one theory, technique or belief system to which I can solely attribute the tremendous spiritual shift that has changed my life. What began as self-exploration and healing via more traditional routes of therapy, evolved via a gateway of meditation and yoga into a deeper desire to understand this universal power that some call God, others call Spirit – I tend to call source. The crux of my discovery? That God is within us all, and when we live and act from that space of infinite power, what we *see* transforms – and so do our lives. For me, heaven is a mindset or state of consciousness rather than a place, and God is a presence rather than a person.

Mine has been a decade-long, ongoing journey of discovery, culminating in a miracle on 28 June 2016. A miracle that shifted my 'beliefs' into conclusive knowing once and for all. But I'll return to that later...

For lifetimes, the majority of us have been living superficially on the upper levels of our conscious minds. We've been milling around like worker ants, completely disconnected and oblivious to the wonder all around us and within, with gut feelings and so-called coincidences hinting from time to time of our innate connection to our power. The noise of our doing and distractions has drowned out the truth about who we truly are. Most of the time we're too numb to feel what's real. Charged by a lifestyle of drugs, coffee, food and technology, we've become addicted to filling each waking moment with something to do. Whether it's work, television or social media, our always 'On' society leaves no space for the discovery of truth. We wear 'busy' as though it's a badge of validity. 'How are you?' they ask. 'Busy', says the stock response, as though the privilege of space and time belongs only to the idle.

We struggle with silence. We find it intolerable simply to sit, undistracted, with ourselves. Preoccupied by the past and constantly predicting the future, bogged down by an insatiable desire to earn more money, drop a dress size, find that perfect partner, become pregnant, secure that promotion, we postpone happiness until one landmark after another is realized. Happiness is elusive, since the goalposts for when we might achieve satisfaction keep changing.

Connecting to our source happens fleetingly when we step outside of our daily lives. It happens when we're jolted by an experience, event or environment beyond our relentless human focus on the body-conscious self. By 'body-conscious' I mean the identity that most of us are conditioned to believe is the sum total of who we are. When we jog and go into 'the zone', when we practise yoga and plunge our focus into our breath – it's there within that space between our inhalation and exhalation that our spirit lies, waiting to connect. Accessing our spirit is achieved through a deliberate effort to shut out the noise of life, literally. Which is why meditation is such a powerful tool. If you find it difficult to start with, as I did, then simply start by practising silence. No books, no tech, no audio, just you and your thoughts for 15 minutes of stillness each morning and evening. It's a practice so at odds with anything we do in our current lives that it'll jolt your mind into preparing for a new habit. Silence creates a space for introspection and for our spirit – which is interconnected to the flow of energy all around us – to be experienced.

Having found this new world, like any ambitious control freak, I attempted to speed and control the process of 'getting it' and becoming this enlightened version of my former self. I embarked on retreats, and weird and wonderful alternative therapies, also attending conferences to broaden my understanding of this new spiritual realm. Day-long silent retreats, healing therapies, I tried them all. For the most part any relief was short-lived. And when old, fearful, saboteur-like behaviours returned, I'd mentally beat myself up for not having changed, for messing up again, ending up feeling like a complete lost cause. I was a relentless perfectionist in the making...

It was an intensive weekend-long course in London that proved to be the critical bridge between the me I'd known until that point and life on the other side. That was where the penny dropped, where the bell tolled and I woke up to the utter falseness of everything I'd believed about my life and myself until that point. It took just three and a half days, which began as what appeared to be a group therapy session, with individuals from all backgrounds utilizing their moment on a small stage in a brightly lit room to share their tale of woe. Pain ranging from failed relationships and resulting loneliness to grief, lives without purpose and a lack of fulfilment despite worldly success, the stories were as varied as they were familiar. Of the 100 people in the room, some shuffled towards the stage to draw us into their troubles, while others cowered from the spotlight, praying they wouldn't be called upon to become visible. And we all watched and listened to other humans just like us open up about their personal torment.

It was a weird parallel universe that first day; the kind of people you might see on the daily commute to and from work but with whom you never make eye contact. Those who sit opposite you in your office and engage in small talk, those you watch on television presenting the news, those you take your post from in the morning, and yet here they were stripped of their disguise, letting us into their most intimate sensibilities.

We heard of parents who'd been absent, abusive husbands who'd cheated and beaten. Evil bosses and co-workers, children lost. From the inane to the incomprehensible, the circumstances spanned the Richter scale. Most people had a story, a comprehension of why they were the way they were, and in every single case, somebody or something was responsible.

Over the course of a weekend too intense and ardent to relay in full colour, we'd all shift from being the victims of circumstance – however horrific – to empowered individuals who accepted what had occurred and were able to distinguish it from themselves. For those who remained in the room throughout that weekend, circumstances became just that – a series of events from which we were detached. Some fled – for the harsh reality is that the stories we tell ourselves are like comfort food. Short-term comfort with long-term implications. And it's these things that allow us a convenient excuse not to activate our greatness. But the reality is that not everybody is ready or willing to let go of their own BS.

For those of us who weaned ourselves of our crutch, a sense of separation dawned on the horizon and a new view, from which it was entirely possible to create ourselves as whoever we chose to be, replaced the fog. It was quite a weekend.

Over the course of those days, I had to discard the old lens through which I'd viewed myself and what had happened, and

I began to occupy a space of neutrality about events in my life. This meant embracing acceptance into all areas of my world and it took time. I began to look at every area of my life in which there was discord. I realized my relationship with my mother was marred by a quiet resentment and pain on my part for the many years of being the child of a woman with an alcohol issue. I began to see my mother for who she was – not as the alcoholic who was too selfish to overcome her addiction so that she might function as the mother we needed, but as a woman who'd experienced and lived with her own pain.

She'd become her pain just as I'd become mine. It was less about forgiving my mum and more about me taking responsibility for having allowed the impact of her dependence – her form of escape – to prevent me from seeing all of the beautiful gifts she'd bestowed on both my siblings and me. The creativity she'd nurtured in us, with the bedtime stories she'd told to rival those of Dahl and Blyton, the weekend trips to every free London museum going and the cultural institutions that stirred our curious young minds. The mere fact she raised us as three children under the age of five, hand-washing our clothes over the bath without a washing machine, carting us from ballet to judo classes on the bus over the years – and all within the context of a strained mind and often volatile marriage. I'd missed all that. So wrapped up in the flipside of the coin and my own self-absorbed (but very human) focus on her dependence on vodka, I'd slandered my mother, reducing her to the villain in my story. With my view of my mother so absorbed by what I'd perceived as her failings, I'd unconsciously put a magnifying glass on the negative – our relationship never stood a chance.

I picked up the phone and I apologized. And a beautiful thing happened. It was like the wall that existed between us began to crumble and I saw my mother with new eyes. I began to enjoy and receive her for who she was, and our relationship blossomed as we began to laugh together.

Then I moved on to ex-boyfriend accountability. Sharp intakes of breath preceded two calls made to suggest a coffee and to issue an apology on the phone, to two men who'd been a part of my life for a season or ten. My calls were unexpected in each case. I believe and hope they brought some sense of peace and understanding to the men who'd loved me. This need for accountability is a staple of multiple spiritual belief systems and it cares less about the behaviour we deem ourselves to have suffered at the hands of another and more about getting us to focus on our own role in causing hurt or distress. We cannot control any other human being, but we can take charge of our reaction to the discord in our past. We can commit to keeping our side of the road clear. In owning my part in the hurt, I cleaned up the murkiness clogging the energetic field and let go of the need to be right or to maintain an ego-driven upper hand. The role of the other person in your conflict is irrelevant – trust that their soul will confront them about that. But in pursuit of the purity of spirit that is your original state, learn to clean up after yourself.

I'm not going to pretend those conversations are easy, but they're essential. When identifying the relationships in our lives that need to be healed, one by one, view it as a sort of spring cleaning and patching-up of your soul; the process of wiping the slate clean in order to build a person who isn't being eaten by parasites of old, eroding remnants of past pain in the process. It's a chance to wind back the clock to a state of nothingness from which everything is possible. Free from the contamination of unconscious stories about who your pain has made you, you can build from this unblemished space with the power of the universe on tap – She-Ra style.

A Life of Meaning

'Changing the world begins with the very
personal process of changing yourself, the
only place you can begin is where you are, and
the only time you can begin is always now.'

GARY ZUKAV

In case you're wondering how doing all this personal development work connects with finding your purpose, be reassured. Our best work always comes from within. Whether your craft is the written word, a knack for design, innovation or delivering a service, when your output is an unadulterated, under-thought outpouring from the boundless well that is within us all, the honesty of your effort will always supersede anything you produce with your thinking mind. Which is exactly why you should act on impulse and intuition. If it doesn't break the law and isn't dangerous, *do* act on those spontaneous pearls that occur in moments of divine inspiration, before life and your thinking mind click back in with thoughts of rationality, fear and distraction from the whispers of your true purpose.

Perhaps you've heard the philosophy 'the answers are within us' and discarded it as tree-hugging fluff. Well, the answers are indeed within us. The problem is that most of us are so clogged up by surviving the impact of lives that aren't working, that we're completely disconnected from the boundless answers within us. Think of it as a detox of the soul in order to get in touch with who we truly are, what we want and where we are headed... For there are moments in our lives when ideas hit us which, if pursued, will change events forever. My father used to call these 'Checkpoint Charlie' moments.

Fast-forward 15 years and I was running my own successful PR agency, when an Indian chef, aged 50 but with the skin and energy of a woman 30 years younger, walked into the office for a PR meeting to explore whether or not we could help her to raise her profile in the UK press.

By this time, I knew exactly what I was looking for in the individuals I chose to represent. Almost two decades of solid graft and a whirlwind of internships and jobs had paid off kindly, and I had a sparkling résumé and career in media. I'd dined with prime ministers, travelled by private jet with billionaires to Monaco, talked dating with Mariah Carey and discussed ethnicity with Meghan Markle (pre Prince Harry), with all the lights, cameras and action it entailed, but there was one fundamental quality that I'd come to require in my clients. A desire that went beyond just ego and commerce. Some motivation bigger than themselves, which we could truly support and champion to the press.

Within minutes I knew the author Anjula Devi was such an individual. She'd raised her children and sent them off to university, whilst simultaneously caring for her autistic sister's kids. In her spare time, she volunteered in special needs schools, using her gift for traditional Indian cooking as a tool to connect with the children, cultivating their self-confidence as they learned to create something beautiful with the ingredients.

Anjula's father, who'd died several years earlier, had been her rock. Her childhood was framed by memories of the bond developed between them over a Masala Dabba and his teachings of the nine key spices intrinsic to every Indian meal, with their various health benefits. She spoke of never having been ill as a child or adult owing to the boosting power of turmeric on the immune system. And she referred to having watched her father override hostility to bring neighbours in their Southall street together by creating a curry with love and distributing it door to door. As she spoke, she lit up with nostalgia – and myself and my team were right back in Southall with her.

Anjula was motivated to take all of the recipes she'd learned from her father and share them with the world in a cookbook that could be enjoyed and embraced by all who read it. Our mission was to assist in raising her profile to the extent that she'd secure a publishing deal and fulfil her dream. By the end of our 90-minute meeting, I knew the news hook wasn't about how to cook Indian food like Anjula – it was something far bigger. Anjula's 'why' was about food's therapeutic ability to unite, connect and empower the individuals who create it. How cooking was the thread between father and daughter – a tool enabling the recovery and rehabilitation of an Indian divorcee, whose decision to separate from her husband due to marital abuse was frowned on by her community, causing her to be shunned. How cooking became a gift to be shared with vulnerable children, to boost their self-esteem, and make them feel capable, confident and worthy.

Creating traditional, authentic Indian food wasn't something Anjula Devi just did – it was the essence of who she was. She'd given us an insight into her personal journey, and how her challenges and successes had evolved into the beautiful chef who now sat before us in our boardroom. For when we show up as who we really are, we are able to connect with people in a more powerful and authentic way. By giving us an insight into who she truly was, rather than just what was written on her business card, Anjula had had a massive impact on us. We'd been moved by her honesty, and we were engaged by her story and sense of purpose. As a result, we became her champions as we bought into her purpose and helped her realize it. For I knew the purity of Anjula's 'why' would be felt by both the media and later, the publishers. As a result, I felt sure they'd go on to offer the woman who was an unknown talent two years ago a book deal and product line, fulfilling the dream that brought us all to tears in the office that day.

So often the business owners and corporate leaders I work with question how they can differentiate themselves in crowded, competitive markets. The answer rarely lies in the function of the business they run or job description they hold. Far more often, it's they themselves and the *way* they do what they do, not what they do, that becomes their walking USP. No one is you, and that is precisely your power.

Success doesn't teach us anything that goes beyond the material world, whereas pain... now that's where we gain our PhD in life. Anjula was indeed a wonderful chef, but it was the spirit of a woman who'd experienced shame, rejection and grief yet stood before us resilient and shining, that we were enraptured by and drawn to.

Pretence is exhausting. There's a selfless power in honest sharing that radiates at the highest frequency. Our truth speaks to the truth in others on a level that transcends typical human conversation, evoking a response in the listener whilst liberating the person sharing. That's a transaction of the highest order. True, free from distillation and preservative, pure communication.

The power of authenticity is your ticket to success, the key to fulfilment, and the investment required is that of being courageous enough to peel off your mask and bravely show up as exactly who you are.

Say Yes to Your Calling

'Your life is always speaking to you. The fundamental spiritual question is: Will you listen?'
OPRAH WINFREY

Flashback 10 years and it was lunch break on a summer's afternoon in 2006 and I had the typical 60 minutes to grab lunch. On this occasion, I hit Oxford Street, Britain's biggest shopping street, to grab a greetings card for my little girl. Aged seven, she was a confident but sensitive little princess, all skinny legs and big hair, which I styled into two tightly curled bunches that stood up proudly, framing her Bambi-eyed face.

Lately, I'd become conscious of her increasing self-awareness. Her class was made up of predominantly white students and she used to come home from school upset because some of the boys in her class were making fun of her. They used to say unkind things like they couldn't see the blackboard because her bunches pointed upwards rather than flowing downwards like Caucasian hair. I was keen to find a suitable princess card that reflected her brown-skinned beauty, in which I'd write: *'You are perfect as you are.'*

What I found was a shop full of shelves packed with cards depicting blonde, blue-eyed princesses. Animated and photographic, almost identical images were printed across every card in the store, apparently oblivious to multiculturalism and the range of customers they might attract in one of the world's most diverse cities. I exited that market-leading card shop and headed to a 'never knowingly undersold' store, now striding more purposefully, with just 35 minutes left of my lunch break, before I returned to my desk at one of London's most prestigious PR agencies, my intern days behind me, for I was now a senior consultant.

Asian cards? Nope. Black cards? None. Surely they'd have cards depicting images of the UK's fastest-growing, mixed-race ethnic group...? Nothing. By the end of my break I'd hit five major shops and discovered the high street was devoid of greetings cards that truly represented the British public. And I was going to do something about it. For my little girl. For all little girls. Without a clue about the retail market, barring my experience flogging handbags and shoes at Russell & Bromley in my teens.

I couldn't have cared less about selling greetings cards, for the margins turned out to be pitiful, but the mission to ensure all children had access to images on cards that reflected their own face was one I felt I couldn't walk away from. I wanted them to be able to validate their identities, with the subtle message that it's wonderful and perfect to be exactly who you are without needing to aspire to a narrow ideal.

It never occurred to me that this gaping hole in the market, which went on to prompt many conversations about diversity, wasn't my mantle to take up. The purpose spoke to me and though many voices would later flood my thoughts, questioning the realism of my ambition, I came alive with this purpose, which was far bigger than myself.

I returned to so-called Showbiz Towers, where million-pound deals and careers were brokered and broken, an entrepreneur in the making. At the time, I had no idea how this source of inspiration, my daughter's beautiful Afro bunches, was about to shift my life into a new gear. But it was a gear of purpose-driven business concepts and creative inspiration, opening me up to another new world, another delicious chunk of living in its roller-coaster process.

A great coach once gave me a golden insight into how she coped with nerves before public speaking events: 'I shift the focus from myself and consider that my job is to help every member of the audience by informing them, to the very best of my ability. I find that thinking about how I can be of service rather than whether or not I'll be received well, causes the nerves to subside almost completely.'

I practised it myself and it works. Even better, I've discovered that if we try to go through life thinking about how we can assist and contribute to everybody we interact with, be it family, friends, in business or the workplace, rather than focusing on what we want to get from these relationships, they improve radically. Having an impact on another person validates our existence, in the way that superficial accomplishments and acumen, money, property and power cannot compare. When we touch the life of another human being, we experience a sense of fulfilment, which I find to be the source of joy in its purest form.

It was the summer of 2006 and the weekend of the Notting Hill Carnival, Europe's largest annual street festival, in celebration of its multicultural past and present, when the first opportunity to realize my dream presented itself. Attracting a diverse audience of over a million people, it's held on the Ladbroke Grove streets where I grew up. Having been acquainted with the vivid colours of the carnival in all its splendour before I could even ride a bicycle, Ann Marie, my business partner at the time, and I decided that the carnival represented the perfect event at which to set up shop and sell our cards to revellers.

It was our first year of trading and the story of this card startup on a mission to put brown faces on card shelves had begun to circulate. We hadn't yet achieved our high-street ambition, but we were selling well online, receiving daily emails of support and thanks from men and women alike, both nationally and internationally, who'd read all about our dream. We were accruing new independent stockists (of which there were many in 2006 before the financial crash put them out of business) each week because our first 16 early designs weren't available in any other shops.

We'd risen before the sun to set up our stall on what seemed a prime Portobello Market spot, nestled between a beer trader, and a jerk chicken and roasted corn stand. Police officers already lined the streets, manning barricades to keep revellers and floats parading uniformly.

By 2:00 p.m, eight hours later, we'd sold less than three cards. Priced at £2 each, we hadn't begun to cover the cost of our lunch, let alone the stall, which had set us back almost £800 for the two-day placement. Our spirits began to sink. While we were encouraged by the smiles and admiration that the images of diverse faces and inspiring captions on the cards were drawing from passers-by, our faith in the commercial feasibility of our first attempt at running a business was wavering. And not for the first time.

The inspiration behind our business, Color blind cards, came from dissatisfaction with the status quo rather than a desire to make a fortune. But the reality was that I was a single mum living in a small housing association flat, dreaming of sending my daughter to private school to secure the best education possible. I was still working full time in my PR day job, writing a monthly column for *Pride Magazine*, and was perpetually knackered from keeping balls in the air and my sanity intact. Color blind cards was a passion with purpose, but it needed to make money. It needed to be worth it.

By 5:00 p.m. we were crumpled. Resigned to the carnival stall having been a disastrous venture, though it went unspoken, our faith in the entire vision had been shaken. Voices of doubt crept in, questioning whether or not the twenty-something business novices who'd invested their hard-earned pay cheque in a big idea were deluded. And then something magical, forever inked in my memory, occurred. A dark-skinned mother and son aged about five years old, whistleblowing and island flag in hand, danced towards our stall, the child stopping in his tracks directly in front of the cards.

'That's me, that's me and that's me,' he said, beaming, as his innocent gaze moved across the images of the child models on the cards, in whom he recognized his likeness reflected.

His mother bought a set, gushing about our brand and the importance of what we were doing. We sold a few more after that, but our pitiful takings had paled into insignificance against the value of that exchange. The power we felt in that moment, the memory of which still lights me from inside, brought back the essence of the *why* that had bowled me over in the department store that day. It was as though in that 10-second exchange my purpose was realized, and the feeling moved me. In that moment, I knew that if we never sold another card, it would be OK. Just to have seen that glint of recognition in his eyes, that unspoken confirmation that he was enough, his skin beautiful and perfect, his identity valid, spoke volumes. But there would be many more moments in that child's life as he grew up when the strength of his self-worth would be challenged purely because of the colour of his skin.

Our cards might have been mere drops in a deep ocean, but they were soul-fuelled, pure, honest and powerful nonetheless. We could have quit that day. Cut our losses and retreated to the security of a company credit card and high-powered media careers, but I couldn't. There was more to come. And while the poor sales from the weekend and a rational head might have questioned the demand for our Color blind cards, something inside me – call it conscience, sixth sense or God – told me my entrepreneurial journey was just beginning.

Somewhere across the Atlantic, 3,400 miles away in a New York City office, America's biggest distributor of greetings cards was surfing the Web, when an article about a 20-something single mum and her multicultural card line caught his interest. He noted the company name and made a mental note to make contact with Color blind cards.

Be the Change

'Not everything that is faced can be changed,
but nothing can be changed that is not faced.'
JAMES BALDWIN

Have you ever noticed how at certain points in your life things seem to flow? How you connect with somebody authentically during a conversation or interaction, and from that genuine connection, possibilities and opportunities are birthed? Just as we were standing at that stall at Notting Hill Carnival, humbled by the depth of meaning and impact our greetings cards had on the children who saw them, distributors in South Africa and America who would go on to enable us to touch the lives of more children on a bigger scale on the other side of the world began to reach out. Call nothing coincidence, for to belittle the power of a force our human minds cannot begin to fathom, is to reject the miracles available to us all in our own lives.

It is this disconnection from our true spiritual nature that sees the vast majority of us miss out on our ability to co-create lives and fulfil our own purpose for being on this planet. We are so out of touch with who we truly are that we forge our identities based on what we are.

For me, the realization that my identity was entirely separate to my true self was one hell of a relief. It was like having a huge painted but tainted canvas wiped clean, giving me the opportunity to see myself and my life with a level of disconnect, and to start over, this time choosing love, integrity and compassion as my crayons of choice. I realize that this concept of not being our identity may sound bizarre, but bear with me and I'll rewind.

We all start out as pure, untainted blank canvases, before our relationships with our parents and those closest to us throughout our life begin to mould us. Our parents' views, behaviours and fears become ours, and it happens unconsciously, so that it's not until we're old enough to step back and consider whether we actually want to adhere to all that we've been taught, that we even begin to question them. We experience disappointment, loss and rejection, storing all of these experiences in our cell memories, so that when another situation occurs that might resemble the former pain, we presume another disappointment or disaster where it doesn't exist. With our focus fixed on this perceived risk, we often manifest exactly that of which we are scared.

As human beings, this is a commonality that binds us. Science itself tells us that energy is transposed and passed on to one another, with good and bad ideas, and ideals about ourselves passed on from generation to generation. It's like we inherit them. For many of us, by the time we're ready to move into adulthood, the boot of our proverbial car is so full of baggage that our vehicle's engine can hardly power up. Knowing this, our task now is to unburden ourselves, one bag at a time. Removing not only our own cases, but also those that were placed upon us. The challenge? To do so lovingly, compassionately, without anger or resentment – bearing in mind that each and every one of us is laden with our own surplus weight. Nobody is to blame and we alone hold the key to our own healing.

A poolside chat on holiday with a girlfriend recently sparked a conversation about how this baggage transference shows up in second-generation immigrants, like the two of us. She shared the story of her mother's arrival from Sri Lanka in the early seventies with two young daughters. She was a qualified anaesthetist and following a divorce from her violent husband, she'd fled the country as a single mum, opting for a better life in a new land. On arrival, she discovered that her qualifications weren't recognized in the UK and so took on menial work before retraining, whilst raising her children alone, without a single family member to lean on for support. The story was not dissimilar to my father's, except that he'd arrived in the UK in the fifties and his qualification was in teaching.

For my generation and the millions of us whose parents came from other lands, we were born into a sense of not belonging that nobody talks about. It's not as though we all sat around the dinner table debating how this existence on the outside of the native 'in-crowd' was subtly impacting our self-esteem and identity – but you'd better believe that it was.

Most of us can recall the feeling of exclusion, whether it's because of the colour of your skin, your sexuality, a disability, your circumstances or the mere fact that you're a woman in a 'pussy-grabbing' world. Multiply that feeling by 1,000, and we might begin to fathom what the immigrants from the Caribbean, Asia and Africa faced when their boats docked and they found their hosts had apparently recalled their invitations. No blacks, no Irish, no dogs. The pain of exclusion is relative, but when you cannot get a place to live or enter a public space because of the colour of your skin, it puts inequality into perspective.

In 1967, Mr and Mrs Loving, whose feat was largely unknown until a Hollywood film broadcast their story to the world, won a landmark civil rights case at the United States Supreme Court, which invalidated laws prohibiting interracial marriage. The state of Virginia argued that it was wrong to bring mixed-race children into the world. Just 13 years after the law was passed, I was born. In 2014, same-sex marriage became legal. Our generation are still being granted *permission* simply to be who we are…

What did rejection and degradation of this magnitude do to the souls of our parents, who were born free but only steps removed from their own enslaved (physically or mentally) grandparents? And still they persisted. But at what silent cost to their sense of self? As the children of parents who were outcasts, that sense of not belonging, of not being enough, was unknowingly dumped in our car by parents with the same (God bless them!) but now even heavier baggage – before we could even speak.

For those of us born to immigrant parents, it showed up as them telling us that we'd need to work harder as a black or Asian person to be successful. Even the way we were disciplined was different... many of my friends experienced 'tough love' to prepare them for a world that their own parents found to be unwelcoming and hostile. Receiving the belt on our bottoms by our father after we'd misbehaved was an occasional but significant punishment in my household and something of a slavery hand-me-down.

On our drive to primary school, my brothers and I had to recite a poem by Henry Wadsworth Longfellow (the education in Jamaica, a British colony until it gained independence in 1962, was heavily Anglicized):

> *The heights by great men reached and kept, were*
> *not attained by sudden flight. But they, while their*
> *companions slept, were toiling upward in the night.*

It sums up part of what my dad felt was required to make a life. *That they while their companions slept, were toiling upward in the night...*

As an adult, I did just that for many years. My best was never enough for *me*.

It goes further back, of course. In the scheme of things, the impact of slavery on black families the world over has only recently become a point of discussion. Like all of the travesties of humankind, if nations were to take ownership and acknowledge their wrongdoing, and seek forgiveness from the groups they victimized and slaughtered, healing could begin. As long as shameful secrets, like humans being reduced to objects for the purpose of commerce and power, continue to be brushed beneath the carpet and factored out of history books and school curriculums, the world will feel the impact of communities pained by wrongdoing. In the meantime, our personal responsibility is to recognize just how deep our roots, and likewise our programming, go. To overlook without judgement the impact of how our cultural experiences trickle into generation after generation, and our individual personas, is to miss an opportunity to better understand both ourselves and each other.

With this understanding, we can decide not to allow any of these predispositions to define us. Then we can deliberately craft new identities not based on labels, stereotypes or false notions about who we are collectively. Instead, we can draw our sense of self from righteous principles and values, and remain firmly focused on the personal legacy we intend to impart on the world. We can make our existence mean something more than the pursuit of our own betterment. We can take full responsibility for who we are.

What I am talking about is the fact that regardless of how much we go through, whether self-inflicted or caused by others, we can choose to allow those experiences to define us and meet pain with pain, or we can choose to be love regardless and create beautiful lives.

Best of all there is little that we need to do to attain this state other than chip away at our hardened exterior and break down our own walls. It's not about morphing into something other than who we are – it's about returning to the truth of who we have always been beneath the wallpaper. Kathi Scott, the UK Director of Nelson Mandela's Children's Fund, did just that – she chose love.

Kathi was born and educated in Northern Ireland at a time when what is referred to as 'The Troubles' were rife. Over the course of three decades, violence on the streets was commonplace, spilling over into Great Britain, the Republic of Ireland and as far afield as Gibraltar. The nation was bruised, women leaders were few and far between and gender inequality was the norm. The product of what is known as a 'mixed marriage' (or two different religions) in Northern Ireland – where Church affiliation reflecting more than just belief and religious bigotry was prevalent – was particularly controversial. Kathi notes that 'In London, you would meet and date someone, and your friend would ask, "What is he?" You would answer something like "He's an accountant." In Northern Ireland, the response was more likely "He's a Presbyterian" or "He's a Roman Catholic."'

Kathi was blessed with wonderful parents whose kindness, decency and compassion made her aware from a very young age that the notion of 'them and us' in all of life's circles – be it skin colour, religion or financial status – was wrong. But outside her world, people were compartmentalized – they went to certain pubs, shops, churches and youth activities, all based on their religion. Because her parents exposed her to 'both sides' equally, it provided the foundations for her to become a champion of social justice. Throughout the last 20 years, she's helped children who've been orphaned through HIV/AIDS, providing counselling and protecting those who've been abused or are at risk of abuse, ensuring that the communities in which they live are stronger in the long term.

Visions are birthed in the heart and mind of someone who's frustrated and tired of the way things are, in contrast to the way they believe things could and should be. Just out of her teens, having decided there would be more opportunities for her to flourish, grow and be comfortable in a more tolerant society, Kathi moved to London. What she didn't expect to encounter was different types of prejudice when she arrived.

In her own words: 'The undercurrents of a notion still existed here, that if you were Irish, or black or poor, you were somewhat inferior, and it was very much a "man's world". I lost count of the times I was denied opportunities, talked down to and laughed at, particularly by men in senior positions. At that point in life, I literally felt all sense of confidence drain from my body.'

The impact was such that even when she'd crafted an exceptional career, going on to serve the charity and Mr Mandela himself, the feeling of exclusion that had been a pre-eminent theme growing up in a separatist society stayed with her, internally putting her right to be at the table into question – imposter syndrome in full effect.

'Have you ever felt like you don't belong, Kathi?' I asked the visionary who sat before me, over a cup of tea.

'All the time,' she answered. 'I still do.'

And yet this strong leader who found her calling aged seven to play her part in combating prejudice, discrimination and racism, works for a charity that helps to improve the lives of up to 100,000 children every year.

'South African actress Dorothy Bernard once said, "Courage is fear that has said its prayers." I've always been determined to retain the kindness and compassion that my parents instilled in me,' says Kathi.

We have the choice to reject society's status quo, whatever our personal experiences of this world have been until today. We can choose who we wish to be both for and within the world, and take action to be part of the change. Kathi's story is testament to that.

In drawing our sense of identity from our connection to our deepest truth – that we are far more than just bodies having worldly experiences – we can approach and handle with divine power the inevitable challenges that impact us all throughout our lives.

The truth will set us all free, and if we consider that mission given a world in dire straits, the quicker we'll all accept that no political knight on a horse is going to save us. All of us can and must be the light and the hero in our own fairytale. How can we be the light? By choosing to live lives no longer led by our heads but informed by our intuition, our spirit.

I believe with every fibre of my being that this is our most pressing work. We don't need any more information – academic or technological – for the time being! We are crying out for the reconnection to our sixth sense and our personal exploration of the wisdom it holds for each one of us. It is this return to ourselves that will expedite our individual and universal world forwards.

As more of us gain the connection of which I speak, our healing will unfurl and the transcendent domino effect of awakening will continue.

Get Soul Conscious

'I am not this hair, I am not this skin.
I am the soul that lives within.'
RUMI

For anybody who might be questioning how all this personal development, introspectiveness and spiritual connection might help you to thrive in the workplace or build a highly profitable business of substance, stay with me – the connection is critical.

The reason for this is that until we come to truly know ourselves, we're operating like cars with a fuel tank near empty. Nowhere near to our full potential. We're like someone before that first cup of tea or coffee in the morning. We function, but fairly inefficiently.

We're a bunch of lunatics who live out our days through a series of reactive interactions controlled by bedlam in our minds. Until we appreciate that all of our understanding and perspective is framed by our previous experience – both our own and that which is inherited – we'll remain prisoners to ideas and decisions based purely on previous events, outcomes and warped points of view.

In my life, this played itself out exactly like this. A series of events – such as growing up in a wounded home, being expelled from school at 15, falling pregnant at 17 – meant I viewed myself as a disappointment and a let-down to the people I cared about, namely my parents. These events meant that I fell out of the educational system, first school and then college, and became an excluded outsider, separate from the world my teenage peers occupied. They were throwing university house parties and I was attempting to master breastfeeding. Add to that the fact I was born into a family of outlier parents – a white woman and a black man, 17 years my mother's senior, who fell in love at a time of great racial tension – and you start to see how the result was a young woman with a serious case of 'I don't belong and I'm not good enough-itis'.

That's the straightforward part. Where it gets more complex is that even when I began to accomplish things light years beyond my own and other's expectations – completing a university degree, toddler in tow, and building a career with all of the awards that came with it – my unconscious view of myself remained stuck in a time warp. While the world no longer viewed me as the expelled pregnant teen, that view of myself as a failure was embedded so deeply into my unconscious mind that it stuck around for almost two decades, long after the cockroach-ridden hostel where I'd spent my pregnant days and after my benefit book had faded almost into another lifetime.

Then one day, when I was about 27, just days after Gordon Brown, the prime minister at the time, had personally handed me an 'Enterprising Young Brit Award', I received a handwritten invitation through the post to visit 10 Downing Street for a round table to discuss how we could create a more enterprising Britain. This was major! It was the sort of event that signalled teary-eyed proud parents and required a good week or two of outfit planning. I was to be one of just 10 individuals in attendance and as it turned out, I was the youngest in the room and one of only two women.

As I passed through security at the entrance to the prime minister's official office, I suddenly became overwhelmed by emotion. I located the bathroom and shut myself in the cubicle, where I took some deep breaths and centred myself. My new reality was such a huge leap from that of my former life that it bowled me over. When I returned to the meeting room to join the table, the conversation began and I recall Peter Jones, one of the Dragons from the *Dragons' Den* TV show, and a senior leader from multinational company GlaxoSmithKline seated either side of me.

Each of us was invited to share our contribution to the question at hand of how we might create a more enterprising nation. I could've said that by gearing up our children from school age to explore and nurture their interests, we could plant the seed of a life built around natural talent, passion and meaning, rather than shoehorning them into a choice of career dictated by the school curriculum or job market. I could've said that incorporating entrepreneurship into the school-day itinerary warranted discussion. But I said neither. What came out of my mouth after the other nine business minds had shared their views were words to the effect of, 'I can be your case study of somebody who messed up and turned it around.'

Despite launching two businesses – which were managing to sustain my daughter's life and mine as a single mum – persuading an archaic retail sector to open its shelves (and mind) to diverse greetings cards and winning globally recognized clients on my PR roster, I still viewed what I perceived as my failures as my most valuable contribution in the room. The reason? Because I didn't feel I deserved to be at that table. I felt entirely out of my comfort zone, a huge imposter. Rather than risk anybody else in the room outing what I perceived as my lack of credence – of not being one of *them* – I dimmed my own light, dumbed down my power and retreated into my safe, cosy, choking teen-mum story.

I don't beat myself up about it – at least not any more – as I'm grateful for the lesson. It's no coincidence that I remember little else from that afternoon beyond the moment I extinguished my own light, and the feeling of defeat. I'd done myself a huge disservice. It's incredible that we can forget decades of memories, but those moments where our consciousness is pricked stay with us, urging us to heed their wisdom or explore what there is to see, lest the same lesson comes around again in a different form.

The only way that we can operate as our optimum, most effective, creative, ingenious and brilliant self, is by working from an enlightened state of consciousness – a new paradigm.

Like a blank canvas of thought that allows us to see the project, conversation or person – including ourselves – before us, without any of the old biased experience clouding our view. If we think we always have the answers purely because we might have experienced something similar at some point in our past, we switch ourselves off completely from receiving new information with an open mind. This applies to people as well as the work and business environments.

Most of the problems in our relationships stem from us being incapable of letting go of old resentments about that thing he or she did last week, last month, last year. We store them up like sins in an attic, so that when our loved ones do anything even vaguely resembling one of their previous fails, we make them pay for all of them. Imagine if you behaved as though you were meeting your boyfriend/husband/boss/mother for the very first time... If you erased all the baggage from the old relationship and just responded to them purely from your experience in that moment, your interaction would be lighter and the relationship would transform. Baggage is a drag.

So how do we get conscious about our thoughts? Becoming aware of the thoughts that show up as preconceptions, judgements, comparisons and limiting beliefs is the first step to winning the exhausting tug of war with our mind. When we accept that our thoughts are predisposed to worry and fear – that they're coming from some outdated version of ourself that's no longer relevant or helpful – and that they aren't our truth, we suddenly have the possibility of entertaining new progressive thoughts. Ones that don't tell you that you can't afford to quit the job you hate or that you'll be alone if you leave your cheating boyfriend.

Eckhart Tolle's book *The Power of Now* was a pivotal turning point for millions, including myself, and he calls it 'becoming the watcher.' When we get conscious enough to become aware of the dialogue in our minds – and begin the process of shifting from lives led by reactive unconscious thought to deliberately choosing the thoughts that are conducive to the reality we're intentionally creating for ourselves – life slips into fifth gear and it's a whole different journey.

Like any ingrained habit, it takes practice to un-train ourselves from lives spent as prisoners to our thoughts. Begin the practice of regularly noticing what that voice is saying about you or your prospects. If it's fear-based – 'I'm no good at pitching,' 'I'm not sure we have the capability to handle this account anyway' or 'My manager has a real issue with me; I'm sure it's because I'm gay' – discard it. Have fun with it! You'll soon notice how your mind loves to replay tired old themes stemming from fear and a place of lack. Instead, choose new thoughts, which will get you into the sort of can-do mindset of progressives. When we think from a centred mind, possibilities become evident.

Every successful athlete has a coach to help them attain their optimal performance and this performance is dictated more by their mindset than their physical aptitude. Be your own coach and take responsibility for your thoughts. They'll shape your world and if you're serious about crafting a life that's the truest expression of who you are, then there are no shortcuts.

Consider that every one of us, regardless of anything that's happened in our life up until this point, can decide today on the kind of person we're going to be. And we can start over. Brand-new fresh page in a crisp new notebook. We can be magnificent. We are magnificent regardless of circumstances or any of the events that might have happened to us in our lives. We simply have to step into our greatness and craft our lives with this untapped power that waits to be unearthed within us all.

At our most compelling, the person that we present to the world must be congruent with the individual we are when we shut up shop. By deciding to stand for something and by infusing our values into every area of our lives, caring in our workplace in the way that we do for those we love, we can stop compartmentalizing our lives. We can make honesty, kindness and integrity values that don't just stop at our front door, but also extend into how we do business, how we treat our co-workers, and how we interact with the Uber driver, the postman, the homeless person. In doing so, we can become whole people creating whole communities, making real change and progress happen in the world.

Taking responsibility for our lives by having the courage to cultivate our inner beauty and power is the first step towards becoming 'soul conscious', enabling us to see both the world and ourselves differently. And we can do this by identifying, acknowledging and freeing ourselves from our weaknesses.

It's impossible to build and sustain a wonderful life from a foundation of untruth. Flaws that remain untackled will seep through the cracks in our lives, eroding its very foundation until it tumbles. One of the great ironies of life is that in a world where we're taught to acquire, our most pressing work should be in peeling back our layers, laying down our 'stuff', and rebuilding from an authentic and whole centre.

Society operates through a series of inauthentic interactions most of the time. I 'meet' the title on your business card and you 'meet' the letters after my name. I become acquainted with your professional seniority and apparent importance, and you become acquainted with my notoriety and social media following. It's a superficial and limited way to communicate, which has nothing at all to do with who we truly are. But imagine just for a moment if I were to park the representative, Jessica, and show you a little of who I am and what I care about, so that you, encouraged by my vulnerability, could park your spokesperson and introduce me to a little of who you are... With preconceptions to one side, the quality of our authentic communication would open up a powerful foundation for all manner of possibilities and opportunities to be created as a result of our genuine connection. Imagine the business we could conduct and the depth of the relationships we could enjoy from that space!

So who are *you*? Just for a moment, lose your representative, your inner publicist who leaps forwards to tell me of your accomplishments, your high-powered role at work or the fact you're the founder of your own business. Or your place as a mother or father to brilliant children, a wife, daughter, husband, whatever. Swipe all of those to the left just for a moment and join me in a quiet moment to contemplate who you are without the badges you wear. Stumped?

I was when my former client and now friend Ali Campbell asked me this question eight years ago. We were sitting in the living room of my flat, in which the shelves were lined with award upon award and framed newspaper articles shouting of my accomplishments... On some level I guess the newspaper clippings were bolstering my self-esteem. Daily visual validation that I was worth something – except the feeling was always short-lived. Short-lived because a) validation drawn from third parties has a shelf life, and b) I was great on paper, but in private a needy and feeble shadow of the woman I presented to the world.

A childhood that lacked stability, followed by years of feeling judged as a school dropout and then a teenage mum, had left me with a point of view that I didn't fit. It stemmed from this deep-rooted feeling of not being enough and not belonging, so whenever I felt my place in the world challenged or that I was being rejected, I felt hurt and reacted with a vicious tongue and irrational action. My inner seven-year-old leaped forwards to defend me from perceived attack. I was a queen at self-sabotage, as family, ex-boyfriends, staff members and my closest longest-serving friends would attest.

I could, and for many years did, build a stellar case for my behaviour, which would generally end with prolific apologizing and attempts to clean up the mess I'd created. But while to disregard my reasons would be to undermine the pride I feel in having taken baby steps towards self-mastery, the harsh, cold truth is that the reasons (excuses) for our ugly just don't matter. Accept that and things get better, quickly.

My life was compartmentalized in those days. Front of house I was doing great work and cared genuinely about making a difference, the better parts of me aching to break free and unleash my power to its fullest potential. But the unconscious point of view that I held about myself kept me shackled. I feared I'd never have the capacity to maintain a happy relationship, and that I'd end up alone and lonely. A fairytale wedding and marriage to a wonderful man who is both my best friend and my greatest advocate is just one major testament to the changes in my life and our ability to create all that we desire if we're willing to put in the 'self' work. Our relationship with ourselves must be tackled before any of our external relationships stand a chance of working long term.

It took me several years to be able to answer Ali's question, so don't beat yourself up if the answer eludes you now. Simply consider that beneath the layers of roles and badges of accomplishment that no doubt fill your social media bios, there's a whole world of you, concerned purely with who and how rather than what we are in the world, that requires your attention. Accepting and trusting in the existence of this divine space, which is separate to the body we occupy, is the first step towards waking up and becoming conscious. Harnessing its power will transform your life, and living from this frequency is a lifelong practice that'll bring you peace, joy and inconceivable rewards. We're never the finished article. I can still be short and defensive, still slip into a headspace where I perceive life as uncertain and unwelcoming, but the difference today is that now I *see* myself rolling in the quagmire of negative and fearful thoughts and feelings. I'm conscious that I've fallen out of alignment and I know that I have the choice to shift my energy back to a higher frequency from which my tranquillity can be restored. Today, even if I'm being judgemental, I see it quickly and consciously decide to return back to the better parts of me. The beauty of this is that like any habit, the more I opt for the light, the easier it becomes to hang out more permanently in this peaceful place.

Unquestionably, my greatest success thus far has been in showing up for the lessons the universe continued to present to me. Lessons that, once learned, left me a bigger version of myself. Expanded, lighter and happier. There have been many times that I have silently chastised myself for this inability to ignore the loud hum of my conscience, calling me to take action. But even if ignored, the hum never goes away. Even when we suppress it under our drug or distraction of choice, the issue that demands to be addressed, the painful conversation that must be had, the frightening decision that must be made – it sits humming, awaiting our attention. Calling us to be courageous and inviting our expansion, growth and healing.

And if you're ready to get deliberate about you, then you'll need to roll up your sleeves and be willing to broach your own set of uncomfortable learnings. It will transform your existence. Through the many small miracles I continue to experience, this warm sense of peace and happiness, which for so long evaded me, is now my default. That is the reward of the journey to self.

Today, I'm careful to seek out the conversations, environments and individuals that allow me to nurture my new serene state of being. I guard my newfound inner peace like a treasured possession, being careful as far as possible not to allow in words, energy or action – mine or others – that threaten to pervade it. That means being mindful of the words I speak, observing the health and intention behind the thoughts that I entertain and choosing the company I keep with care. I let my intuition guide my life in a way that I never did before. No conscience niggle goes ignored, and equally, from this connection to spirit, I am receptive to the energy of the people and places around me in a way that acts as a compass, constantly directing the path I take in my life.

Most of us rarely, and some of us never, tap into this incredible centre point – our soul, source, essence, God – whatever terminology feels right. We're so consumed with living our day-to-day lives and trying to make 'stuff' happen, constantly moving from action to distraction, that we've become disconnected from our own truth. A truth that would allow us to co-create our lives with the kind of divine power and support no business school, degree or mentor could ever compete with – if only we could connect with it. Connected to our divine source, we would experience what it is to have our lives flow.

Leap!

*'The state of your life is nothing more than
a reflection of the state of your being.'*
WAYNE DYER

So are you ready to roll up your sleeves and sweep out your internal cobwebs? Are you willing to walk into the fire, knowing that the door to escape captivity lies open, just beyond the flames? Can you sacrifice certainty for the promise of nothing – and yet everything?

As you move into soul consciousness it becomes impossible not to question the state of your life and the decisions you're making. If you aren't living your truth, and are simply surviving and tolerating, rather than relishing your life, be it in your work or your relationships, a feeling of conflict starts to bubble within you.

Often, we tell ourselves that we don't know what's for the best, because the answer lies in the option that demands more than we're actually required to give or do. We say we aren't happy in a job, but don't have the courage to quit that regular pay cheque and promised pension for fear that we won't be able to create financial security for ourselves. We say we want to lose weight, but lack the willpower to change our lifestyle. We say we're tired of being single, but are unwilling to consider how our own vibe and way of being might be preventing us from attracting love. Rather than confront the cold, harsh reality that *we* are the ones holding back from achieving our own happiness, we create magnificent stories to deflect and distract us from the truth. Anything to justify the fact that we're not prepared to do what's necessary. We refuse to confront that critical truth and so, trapped in our own BS, we chase our tails, hamsters in wheels, burrowing around despite there being an exit sign marked as clear as daylight.

It's always fear that stops us from doing what's required. It's amazing to observe how often we make our own pain and unhappiness a security blanket, as though living a life that's limited somehow protects us from exposure. There's a feeling of safety in playing small. In having a high-powered job title at a firm you hate working for, in being professionally successful but overweight, in being happily married with kids but unfulfilled. We cap the possibilities for our lives because beneath the pretence, the truth is that few of us believe we're worthy of becoming the complete badasses that we're meant to be. Partly because we don't love ourselves nearly enough and partly because society conditions us to think that discontentment is somehow normal.

Have you ever looked at the misery on the faces of the people doing the rush-hour commute to work in the morning? It's as though they've all been drugged into apathy and acceptance of mediocrity or worse, misery. We live for the weekend and two-week holidays, clinging on to unhealthy relationships for fear of who or what we might become if we were to leave, plastering over the sadness of an unfulfilled life with whatever vice takes the edge off...

You *know* you want different. You know *this* is not it; it can't be! And yet you're clueless as to what it's all about, what your life purpose is. Or perhaps you have a niggling, possible purpose in the waiting, that world-renowned blog, social enterprise project, book, business idea that's been floating around your head and heart for ages... And yet you haven't had the time, cash, motivation (delete as appropriate) to get started. Excuses being because you have an important day job/three children/social media habit that keeps getting in the way of that thing that deep down you're yearning to undertake.

All of the aforementioned may well be true. But the reality is that what you have here is a catalogue of reasons excusing you from taking responsibility for your life. Recounting all of the reasons that leave you powerless to do that which you long to is lunacy. And if you're ready to shift from a mindset of victimhood that leaves you floating down the stream allowing life to happen to you, to an empowered existence in which you take deliberate steps to create the kind of life you're meant to live, then you must first accept that you're responsible for every element of your existence. From the goldfish in its bowl that needs feeding each day, to the Monday-morning commute that leaves us feeling drained, to the man or woman we want sharing our bed – we chose and manifested it all. And it all started with our thoughts. Nothing in existence is possible without it first having been a thought. It's a fact spouted often, but when we pause long enough to digest it, it's impossible not to accept our true level of responsibility for our circumstances and the lives we've created.

Taking responsibility is a game-changer. It frees us from self-imprisonment and releases the object of our blame from being our scapegoat. While being accountable might be uncomfortable, it puts us back in the driving seat of our lives. It makes us active rather than passive players. With responsibility comes new possibilities for learning, growth and healing. The day I took responsibility for my part in the failure of my past relationships, I stopped being a victim of both the heartache and the fallout. I accepted that my most painful relationships had served valuable lessons, enabling me to emerge a braver version of myself. I accepted that my own lack on consciousness had contributed to the disharmony. I accepted that I hadn't known how to love myself and so therefore I was ill-equipped to love another. I also accepted that I'd unknowingly chosen relationships that would magnify the very areas of myself that needed spiritual attention.

When I was needy and lacking in self-worth, I attracted men who magnified these feelings of loneliness by being emotionally unavailable and incapable of intimacy. They would lean out as I would lean in, leaving me desperately trying to be whatever I could to reassure myself that I was enough for him. Full makeup, expensive blow-dries, beautiful shoes, constantly 'done' up, it was an exhausting treadmill! In those days, my happiness was almost entirely outsourced, and as time went on and my desperation worsened, the self-worth I'd built up through my career wasn't enough to feed my ego's desire for external validity. I had many moments when I'd question how I came to be that sad woman who searched emails and text messages for evidence of betrayal – often finding exactly what my focus sought. Mostly, however, I was unable to give myself the love I desired so badly. And I felt lonely.

I'd always wanted to get married. Not for the fairytale dress or the wedding bash to remember, but purely to skip the event to the happily married stability part afterwards. The bit where you're intertwined with a person who becomes your reliable forever. So that decisions would no longer be mine alone to make, and where family days out at the park involved two adults, as did carving the Sunday dinner. The important stuff. Having been that young, single mum who rocked up to parents' evenings alone or with her own father most years, I now wanted a turn at playing happy families, at acting out what I saw as 'normality'.

I've been fortunate to both receive and give much love in my life. And no matter how fierce the burning desire for marriage and stability with a partner, the realist part of me cannot pretend that areas of my relationships that weren't working didn't exist. The inconsistency of my personal life leaked its way into every area of my existence, depleting me as I clung on desperately for what I thought I wanted. It was like paddling upstream through fierce waves and it was exhausting. When I finally lost all fight and became depleted, it was all I could do to curl up in a ball and yell, 'I surrender!'

Eventually, my sadness became dark and threatened to drag me under. I'd sit on the balcony, cigarette in hand, and look at the moon, asking if somebody 'up there' could extract me from the relationship, because I didn't have the courage to do it myself. Feelings of rejection and despair at being unable to 'make' my relationships work left me unhinged. I would cut up clothes, smash plates, generally out of control and angry – mostly at myself. It was ugly behaviour, defining me, or so I thought at the time.

The reality was that I'd been desperately holding on to a love that was no longer meant for me. The universe was serving me a big wrenching shove out of the door and yet, stubbornly determined to make my relationship work, I held on for all I was worth.

On one occasion, I discovered an email exchange between a bathroom sales assistant and my then boyfriend. From the conversation, it was evident her style of post-sale customer service went way beyond that of just checking the shower was functioning. The madness mist descended on me. Worst of all, her advances clearly hadn't been curtailed. On the contrary, the flirtatious email suggested the post-sale service was just getting started.

The madness mist I refer to is a relic of the old me and it used to come over me when I felt my control around my life was slipping away. I'd go into saboteur mode rather than allow it the freedom to combust of its own accord. I'd do anything to be in control, even if it meant blowing myself up in the process, such was the intensity of my anger.

So one morning after barely an hour's sleep, as my mind churned over the perceived deceit, I dropped my daughter off at school, kissed her goodbye and drove straight to the bathroom showroom where the saleswoman worked. My anger was geared at this woman, who was quite likely oblivious to my existence and in any case, owed me nothing. It was easier to hate her. Hating him would have meant that I had to take responsibility for staying. And I was not yet brave enough to leave. I jumped out of my 4×4, water bottle in hand, and strolled into the store. I can't remember what I said to this poor, unsuspecting woman, who at quarter to ten in the morning would just have begun her day. But I poured the entire contents of a litre bottle of water over her head.

Yes, people, my crazy gene runs deep. I do everything with gusto, insanity included. I'm not proud of my behaviour today, though. I cringe at the thought of how I turned on my heels and strutted out. I soaked her – of course I did – messing her makeup and blow-dry. But if I'm honest with myself now, the only person I was really destroying in those days was myself. It wasn't her that I hated, it was me.

A couple of days later, when the mist had subsided, the gravity of my sabotage and the lunacy of my actions became evident. I returned to the store with a huge bouquet in hand, looked her in the eyes and asked for her forgiveness. The extremity of my behaviour illustrates who I was, then. Utterly lost, afraid, and after years of suppressing layer upon layer of unaddressed pain, I was falling apart.

Then one day something inside me shifted. My prayer was answered and I found the strength to extract myself. It was then that I walked out of the door for good, piecing myself back together, over time, drawing huge strength from having leaped into the realms of self-sufficiency and emotional independence. And so in my empty flat, where I slowly began to put together my broken pieces, I discovered that there's nothing more liberating than walking away when the soul is compromised.

But it wasn't easy. I didn't have the vigour I once had as a new 18-year-old mum. Now, I was looking ahead to another 18 years of childrearing alone and even the thought of the road ahead exhausted me. But while my body and mind were weak, there was a sense of peace in my heart and in my home. I'd courageously given up the fight and without knowing it, I'd stepped into my truth, handing my load over to the ultimate force. Relief and a sort of calm reassurance that all was as it should be were palpable.

Sometimes you have to break your own heart in pursuit of your truth. But the wonderful thing about life is that as you face your fears and addictions—whatever it is that's plastering over your sense of lack, be it food, alcohol, drugs, a career or a man – you emerge with new power. Often, we replace one addiction with another and I found the hardest thing was just sitting with myself on those nights, children in bed, silence echoing through my flat. Dreams and plans for the presumed future now crumpled memories, replaced with uncertainty and a blank space.

In the darkest hours I felt I'd failed, but the truth was that I'd stepped into the light. What I perceived then was that I was in the midst of a breakdown. I felt as though I were in a cyclone, as the stability of having a routine and a stable home had been uprooted by my decision to walk away from my reality as it was. In fact, I was actually having a life *breakthrough*, and beneath the pain and sadness was this sense of peace, a silent calm. When we're brave enough to make the hardest choices, when we can step up to the challenge and do that which our soul tells us must be done – rather than shy away from this truth for an 'easier' option – the universe rewards us for our integrity, courage and lessons learned.

The critical juncture – should I stay or should I go? There are no two ways about it; being at the helm of your own life ship isn't always a smooth sail. When you have a job, you have a guaranteed wage, most likely a benefits package and some financial security. Your day will often end – depending on the industry and your level of seniority – when you leave the premises, at which point your mind is left free to wander and focus on your other responsibilities and interests until the following morning. You have other people to lean on – a support group of colleagues. You might even have an internal network to empower and nurture your progress through the ranks. You also often have 20 days' holiday, an hour's lunch break, a set time to be at your desk – a desk in an office you didn't choose. Limitations. Rules. Office politics. Rush hour. What you have is a huge chunk of your life being decided and designed by another person or people – and *their* design may or may not be the best environment in which you can flourish.

It's not that I believe that entrepreneurship is for everyone, and being an employee can be wonderful. The years I spent working for others opened up the world to me, providing the perfect landscape in which for me to acquire skills, contacts and an understanding of the media industry. I learned how to work within teams and gained all sorts of other important transferable skills, which have aided my growth, and I'm forever grateful for the spark that my bosses saw in me and nurtured. If you like, I grew up in the companies I worked for. But there came a point when it was no longer possible for me to pursue the life I wanted for myself – the greater version of myself with a bigger life – within the confines of my jobs. At that point, I leaped *towards* my vision rather than numbing that inner desire and telling myself all the reasons why it would be ludicrous to leave. This is the critical juncture.

My thinking mind told me that in my swanky PR job, there were all sorts of benefits. We got to be ferried around London in Mercedes Benz cars for lunches with journalists at Nobu and Hakkasan, which the press paid for, for a start – and I *love* Japanese food. Who would give that up? My thinking mind told me that if I wasn't Jessica who worked for the influential company I did then the editors who took my calls might decide not to when I was no longer working for them. My thoughts screamed all sorts of fears about the fact I had no idea how to run a PR business, no team, and that without a Bond Street office on my business card, who the hell was I?

People rarely ever left our agency. It was a very nice gig. And yet all of the reasons to stay didn't outweigh the fact that my heart and soul had outgrown my role as a PR consultant in said swanky firm. I'd caught up with my potential and more awaited. I wanted the freedom to be a fully involved parent, so that I didn't miss out on attending another of my daughter's school assemblies. Where I could work on my own terms, setting my own hours. Where my job worked around my life and parental responsibilities, creating a work–life balance. I wanted to see if I could do it alone, to challenge my own capacity. I needed to get creative with my life. My soul was calling me to inch towards the next stage of my life and this manifested itself in moments where I'd feel a huge disconnect from the superficiality of this media world in which I was ensconced.

Launching Color blind cards and realizing that I could create something that major stores actually sold to real customers – who were strangers and not just friends making a pity purchase – in random places like Bermuda, gave me confidence in how awesomely unexpected life could be. I saw that I could create something that made a difference, which touched people on the most real and authentic level. So aged 28, still a single mum with peanuts in my savings account but a purse full of purpose, I resigned from my sweet pay packet and set up on my own.

Within a month, I was bringing in three times my salary and had two household names on my roster. I went on to live far beyond my means, enrolling my daughter in private school and making a hash of my business finances. But even through the mess and by making mistakes – lessons – I built a life of freedom and sustained it. And what an incredible course in self-development running a business has been. The net *does* appear when you leap, people. When you're doing what you're supposed to be doing, doors open. You have to love yourself enough and believe in yourself enough to explore what your soul calls out for. And as you plunge into whatever it is that you were created to do, you start to flow...

When we take full responsibility for our lives without blame or resentment, we gain complete clarity about what must be done. If you're ready to shift into your next phase, an exciting new chapter of your life, then it's time to leap. Just leap! It's as simple as that. If you want to sing, sing. If you want to blog, blog. To start a business? Start it right now. Observe your thoughts, as your voice of fear clothed as rationale will jump forwards with a catalogue of reasons why it's not that simple. But having worked with hundreds and hundreds of would-be entrepreneurs through my workshops over the years, I've found many are waiting for permission and a suitable moment to spread their wings. Newsflash: it's *never* going to be the perfect time.

In the Western world, we're fortunate to have huge access to trillions of books on practical steps and support when it comes to launching a startup or sideline project, but in them there's no recognition that you're not your job title. Realizing your worth isn't your pay packet is the first step to freedom. *You* aren't the sum of what you do or what you have. Who we *are* is our personal truth, and we all have an obligation to quieten the noise of jobs, roles and responsibilities long enough to get in touch with the calling that's just waiting to be given the space to reveal itself. It doesn't matter one bit what occupation or purpose is calling you forth. It matters only that you're doing exactly what lights up your soul.

Suppressing it leaves us unfulfilled, living a lie and ultimately sick. So batten down the hatches – for the adventure stepping into the next phase of your life is always going to require a courageous core. Take comfort in the fact that when we embrace our God-given reason for being on this planet, the universe kicks into action and will support us at every juncture for as long as we stay connected to this source power. It's a hell of an adventure, so leap!

Project You

'We are all on this earth for a unique special purpose, our job is to discover what that is.'
DEEPAK CHOPRA

Ready to leap but perturbed by the absence of an end goal or a plan? Unsatisfied, unfulfilled, but know your current life isn't your purpose?

The truth about our purpose lies in each moment. If the destination and the end goal evade you, simply follow the small things that light you up. Wherever you feel awe, fulfilment and joy, go there. Whoever leaves you feeling inspired and ignited, spend time with them. Whatever it is that tells you that you're unequivocally alive is what you must spend time doing – even and especially if it bears no relevance to the life you've crafted for yourself. The biggest disservice you can ever do to yourself is to compromise on your own truth and calling. So even if you've built a life in which you now feel you no longer fit, it's not too late to begin chipping away at it until you're standing naked, ready to rebuild an existence that honours your true self.

An unloved life is insanity while a value-driven, soulful way of working and living, in which we step into our true calling, is the prize. Change is coming and we're the spiritual warriors forging the way. More people than ever are becoming purpose-driven entrepreneurs or infusing 'intra-preneurship' into their workplace. One by one, we're waking up.

If you're one of the many walking around with that idea or passion that you dream of bringing to fruition, know that you've been gifted with that idea because it's your purpose to bring it into realization. Nothing is an accident. Your vision is valid and you, brilliant person, are perfectly placed to make it happen. No soul-calling comes without the support of the ultimate source as your mentor. The universe has your back. You only need to respond to the call to action that your ideas and inspiration present. The rest will reveal itself in good time. Show up for the challenge by creating the space to let your plan formulate. Break the plan down into small, bite-sized, entirely do-able chunks and then begin. Just begin.

When I was a child, my mum used to take my brothers and me on what she called 'magical mystery tours'. They'd take place on the weekends or in school holidays, and meant an early start with packed lunches of sandwiches and fruit, with my two brothers, Mum and myself boarding a bus to an unknown destination. We'd have no idea what part of London we were headed to or what our destination was – and that was the magic. The surprise, generally a museum or an undiscovered park, was always good fun, but the journey with a mystery destination was the exhilarating part. This is what life should be about. A journey in which the trip itself is full of wonder and the focus on the destination is released.

This doesn't mean that we don't create goals. It's crucial to evolve your fuzzy aspirations into goals with a clear path of steps that need to happen, in order for the goal to be realized. Then it's down to us to get deliberate about our lives, by taking consistent action repeatedly, until the pursuit of our goal becomes a habit. In that action, confidence and a healthy new view of yourself as a 'doer' emerges. Possibilities open up and an inner fire is sparked. Most people never move from goal to habit – but you're not most people.

Truth has a way of cutting through noise. Many years ago, I recall having sent my friend Jodie a text message to cancel our planned meet-up. It might have been a yoga class I was bowing out of, a coffee or a cocktail – I don't remember. But I could feel my friend's understandable annoyance at my cancellation as she responded with a curt acknowledgment. It wasn't the first time I'd bowed out of an arrangement last minute, so when I next saw the woman, who's been much like a big sister to me over the past decade, I was sheepish. Ever wise, her words penetrated my BS and remain with me to this day. 'It's just that when you flake on me, you flake on yourself.'

Now I was a doer, a doer on speed, in fact. My insatiable appetite for professional accomplishment to fill my lack meant that I never flaked on work. But in the areas of my life that were just for me, the me beneath the roles and uniform, my dedication waned. On many occasions when I made a plan to socialize, attend a non-work event or do a yoga class, I flaked, last minute. I let down whomever I'd made the arrangement with, but most critically neglected to give myself the importance I deserved. Her words struck me like a bull's-eye, and from that day I've viewed with new importance both my word and my commitment to show up for myself, to value my downtime, with the same reverence as my external engagements. When we make even the smallest of compromises, it becomes easier and easier for it to become a commonplace habit. As flaking on ourselves becomes our standard, we lose touch with who we are and what we stand for. We end up flailing around in the wind with life blowing us from left to right, rootless human beings uncommitted even to themselves. And it's a destabilizing way to live.

I haven't perfected the balance, as self-preservation and honouring ourselves is just another habit to be developed and practised. The key is to develop a level of awareness and questioning around why we make the choices that we make, rather than hiding behind statements like 'I have nothing to wear.' How we treat our downtime, our bodies, our money, and those we love and care for, says everything about how much, or how little, we love and honour ourselves.

It is within this endless questioning of our constructed selves that we can unpick the knots that prevent us from making real progress in our lives, moving us closer to our personal vision for the individuals we wish to become. In order to lead the lives we want, we must develop a burning desire fuelled by our *why*. Within the depth of character that develops as we detangle from false narratives about who we are, and the limiting beliefs that come with them, clarity and effectiveness emerge. And when the world and its superfluous distractions cloud this perception of the ultimate us, meditation is just one of the tools that I personally have found essential in helping to plug me back in to my truth and remind me what I'm really up to with my life! I can't recommend it enough. Start with two minutes, or five minutes if you can. I recommend a daily practice, as consistency is more important than the length of time you spend doing it. The start of the day is a great time to set intentions for that day, rather than rolling into it reactively. Night then becomes a precious time for regrouping.

Deciding to show up for 'you' is the greatest gift you can give yourself. Get deliberate about the life you intend to create and fill your world with reminders of who you're on a mission to become. Dedicate a day to creating a vision board filled with words epitomizing the character you're transitioning into and the life you're creating. Switch off your phone. Indulge yourself in the moment and whatever awakens the part of you that sits quietly within, awaiting remembrance. For in the escape, your truth will emerge.

Let words like love, abundance, honesty, leadership, contribution – whatever strikes a chord – accompany images of the world you're creating for yourself. Gift *you* with the space to throw yourself into this unapologetically creative task. Tear images from magazines that warm your soul, letting them cover a large page, just for you. Write a personal statement outlining your vision for yourself and your life, spelling out your goals both personally and professionally. Get detailed with your statement and include adjectives that describe how you want to feel as this best self you're moving towards. Include practical points about what you're creating. If it's making your first million that appeals, ask yourself why. Perhaps it's for freedom and financial security... Then let those words sit alongside your goals on the page in granular detail. Position your statement and vision board somewhere prominent, where you'll see it each day before you rise and before you rest your head. Be mindful that if others are going to see your statement, their own limiting beliefs might cause them to undermine your vision for your greatest self. Those who haven't yet recognized their own innate power will either be inspired by yours or feel threatened by it. Shine your light regardless. Dimming it to make others comfortable does you both a disservice.

Flood your psyche with the vision of the person and life you're growing into, and commit to taking responsibility for all that you consume from this day onwards. Watch the company that you keep. Do conversations with your friends and partner leave you feeling lifted or drained? Does the media you watch and read leave you inspired and learned or depressed? Give your brain clear messages through visual and audible reminders of where you're heading, providing your soul with the food that will support its growth.

Often, showing up will mean leaving people behind. When we show up for ourselves, it has a phenomenal effect on those around us. Depending on where their own sense of self is at, it will either empower and inspire them or leave their own feelings of inadequacy heightened. When we see others shine by pushing the boundaries in their own lives, it casts a spotlight on our own behaviour, leaving us questioning our own way of being and what we're doing – or not doing – with our lives. This isn't your issue to manage, because the best thing you can do for anyone is to become the greatest you.

There may be feelings of resentment, bitterness, even suggestions that you somehow think you're better than others as you shed your old skin and begin to change. Change is disconcerting for people, but this 'stuff' belongs with the individuals not yet awake to the brilliance of their own light, those still caught up in holding others responsible for where they find themselves. Don't take it on. Work hard to keep your own energy field clear with feelings of love and empathy for the people in your life who are still shackled by their own shit. Don't make it about you – it's never about you. I've found that loving people when they're unkind, along with moving from anger and resentment to forgiveness – even though it's often from a distance that allows self-preservation – continues to be the greatest exercise in humility. It's like weightlifting for the soul. A chance to flex your muscles and emerge in better shape.

In the past year Audible has become my best friend. I've devoured no less than 15 audiobooks in a matter of weeks just on my commutes into the office, by authors whose message is aligned with the life I'm creating for myself – from the late, great Louise Hay and Wayne Dyer, to my inspiring publishing house peers Gabrielle Bernstein and Rebecca Campbell, along with legendary writers Chimamanda Ngozi Adichie, Maya Angelou and James Baldwin. While the content might differ, all of these writers share high-frequency messages of expansion, enlightenment and reflection. Morning 15-minute online yoga sessions and 'quotes of the day' ping into my inbox each morning. And then, of course, there are the nightly gratitude lists and the personal statement – the reminder of the life and woman I'm evolving into, which I come face to face with twice each day. Transformation is something of a standoff with the unenlightened you, and our ego craves the security of our old diminishing habits and mindsets. To defeat it, to truly show up for ourselves, to change and grow, we need ammunition.

Gear yourself up with a dynamic spirit reticent in its determination, so that when it comes to the conflict, your truth, the god or goddess that you were created as becomes the last individual standing.

One of my dearest friends, Ruki Garuba, has been a stylist to superstars for over a decade. We met whilst working on the editorial team of a magazine over 15 years ago when we were both in our early twenties. Soon after, she left for LA in the USA in pursuit of an adventure and a new life. She met a guy in a band, fell in love and adapted to life as a fully fledged Californian girl dressing some of the world's biggest music stars. She spends her life travelling the globe, staying in the finest hotels, has acquired an admirable following for her fashion blog and is highly respected for her achievements in the fashion world. It's a fairytale life, except that my friend's story is not yet complete.

Having been on her own mind, body and spiritual journey as a young woman who leaped through her own fear to start a new life alone on the other side of the world, she has now reached a point in her life where she's itching for more and for something different. Fashion is great, she says, and yes, it pays handsomely, but she wants, no *needs*, more. My friend, who has the most beautiful, calming, empowering presence, has a dream of helping her clients beyond their wardrobe choices. She wants to help people overhaul their diets and lifestyle choices, to make them feel fit, healthy and happy. She wants to impact lives beyond aesthetics and make a difference – but 15 years into her cushy career as a superstar stylist, she's buried this desire in her Louis Vuitton carry-on bag.

We met in a beautiful European city for a girly weekend to reconnect, and fresh pasta and several glasses of wine later, we were discussing her vision as she recounted the reasons she hadn't yet made the leap into this new zone. Later that night, I was invited to watch her client perform to an audience of 20,000. I sat side of stage and as the evening went on, my jaw dropped in awe. My girlfriend of 15 years wasn't a stylist – she was running the freaking show! By putting her client at ease as she ensured he was in the mental and spiritual space to light up the stadium, she brought joy to thousands. She didn't *want* to be a lifestyle coach, she was already doing it – she just hadn't made the shift in perception in her own mind or given the service she was clearly already offering the new title it warranted!

We discussed this the next morning at breakfast and I told her that what I saw was a woman who was effortlessly easing into her new chapter from the most authentic space possible. She was offering the very service with such purity of heart that it had already positioned her as an integral part of his team, having a massive impact on her client. While she might not yet boast the label of a 'lifestyle guru' or be charging her clients as such, this formalization of her exciting next chapter would follow effortlessly as soon as she made the shift in her perception in her own mind. She needed to stop doubting herself and step into her greatness.

When our head gets in the way of our desires, we start overthinking and trying to box things into the way they *should* be, or the way other people or society say things should be. But when we act from our heart's desire and utilize our God-given gifts, we tap into the support of the universe, which is the greatest of all mentors. Standing outside of my girlfriend's life, I could see clearly that she was indeed moving towards her goal and her next chapter, but for her it felt as though she were in Groundhog Day, reliving the same events and making little professional progress.

The lesson for us both was that she'd already done the most critical part of her transformation – she'd simply started, no permission needed. If you want to be a leader and create change in the world, then be a leader and create change in your family, your workplace, your local community – don't wait to be handed the White House. If you want to be the world's leading activist blogger, then don't wait for an audience of millions, get on camera now. Don't wait for permission or for what you perceive to be the perfect set of circumstances to get started. Start today, now, taking small actions towards becoming the person who occupies the life you desire for yourself. Act like you've already become the person you wish to be. It really is that simple.

Every little thought we have or action we take will lead us either towards that ultimate goal or away from it. In every interaction, we can lift the conversation or pollute it. No matter how limiting your current circumstances seem, or how cavernous the distance between your reality and your desire, your journey across the bridge to the greatest you can still begin. All you have to do is start right now to entertain the idea that the biggest barrier between your today and your tomorrow is in your ability to see yourself in that future and *not* external factors contributing towards it. Your outlook and perspective are everything. Perspective is the fairy dust that shifts a no-hope situation into a new realm, from which possibilities are revealed.

That redundancy that came unexpectedly out of nowhere is the lifeboat ready to carry you to the pursuit of your passion. Your heartbreak is a pivot to reposition you towards an even greater love. The traffic is a chance to dive into the audio track holding a message that might just change your life. Single parenthood is a golden ticket to an unbreakable maternal bond and unbridled strength. Selecting our perspective isn't, however, as simple as opting for a positive mental attitude. It's a strategic tool for living a life that works. When we decide an event or situation is negative, we box ourselves into submission and we deflate. Our point of view about any and everything determines our life and what shows up in it – choose it wisely.

Arrest Your Habits

'Self-trust is the first secret of success.'
RALPH WALDO EMERSON

Your vision of the great, powerful and loving human you're transitioning into being is becoming clearer. You're preparing to step into greatness. Your greatness – that ultimate version of you and your life. The person who has leaped beyond their fears is facing their ugly, unloading their baggage and conquering their limiting thoughts. Becoming a person who is newly conscious of the universal power we can connect with, generating a space from which we can live and create, where exploration is the most fulfilling and delicious adventure of all.

I used to think that becoming conscious was something I could learn and tick a box. That I could accomplish it in the same way I'd learned my theory to pass my driving test or done years of internships to secure a career in media. But that desire was just my ego talking again. As I continue down this beautiful road of spiritual awareness and self-discovery – for they are one and the same thing – each time I think I've nailed the shift from my old way of being, the universe stops me in my tracks. The late spiritual guru Wayne Dyer describes it as the 'afternoon of our lives', where ambition driven by ego is replaced by a desire for a meaningful existence. And the universe sends me a lesson that tells me that my ego – ego meaning identification with my physical rather than soul existence – has once again got in my way. Consciousness is not to be attained – it's to be allowed.

Unlearning our old way of being and replacing the very common human presumption that we need to 'make stuff happen', that we alone are responsible for the way our life turns out, is not an overnight job. For a control freak like me, developing a faith that meant I could outsource the responsibility for my life's work to a higher power was a scary prospect at first. You might have picked up this book with the expectation that it might inspire or motivate you to fulfil a predetermined goal or life plan that you've been sitting on. And I'm not suggesting for a moment that you should throw away your dreams and plans. Instead, consider that there's likely a plan for your life, a purpose for your existence that goes beyond your limited periphery. A purpose so huge it sees you live the sort of fulfilled, joyful life that not only benefits you, but also contributes to the world.

We only know what we know, right? So the only way you can ever experience the euphoria of seeing the divine plan for your life unfold is by loosening the reins around your existence. By letting go of expectation and allowing the universe to do its sublime, kick-ass thing. A leap of faith? Yes. But moving from fear to faith doesn't mean you stop taking action in your life. On the contrary, as your connection to your inner power develops, you'll begin to see miracles unfold in your life, like signposts reassuring you that you're on the correct path and are indeed being guided. Trust me – you'll experience opportunities and connections showing up at the perfect time you need them. You'll bump into people you were just that moment talking or thinking about. You'll see signs everywhere. In short, your life will stop feeling like it's an uphill struggle with you against the world and you'll find it starts to flow.

When this divine intervention shows up, don't write it off as coincidental. Accept with grace that you're being supported and guided to your greatness. Each time you smile knowingly as an email pings into your inbox at the very moment you were considering calling that contact, your faith will grow and your spiritual connection deepen. You'll be one step removed from your former faithless existence and closer to living your true purpose, doing your divine work.

In the months leading up to me resigning from my job at the PR agency, I'd begun to feel a compromise with the values of honesty and integrity that I'd been raised with. I'd become disillusioned with this superficial world of 'kiss and tell' newspaper stories in which I didn't feel I belonged. At first the discomfort was mild, and I justified my presence at the company through the fact that my personal role didn't involve the sale of stories that often wrecked the lives of other people. But as I grew from my mid- to late twenties, the hum of my conscience became louder and a news story about television's biggest reality show became the catalyst for my resignation.

While my head understood that interviews with a young celebrity with a terminal illness commanded a hefty price tag, my spirit found it hard to come to terms with showbiz media's preoccupation with the desperately sad story that was unfolding of a young family's pain. The magazines and newspapers published these stories because they sold copies, but I couldn't continue to be part of that media machine. It's not that I judged anybody involved in the equation – I just felt a strong sense that it wasn't where I was meant to be. That world seemed false and soulless. It was 2008 and looking back, my awakening was beginning. Had I not responded at that time by resigning from that cushy position, I've no idea how much longer it would've taken before the universe presented me with another opportunity for a consciousness upgrade.

When we're ready to receive our education, the teachers show up. One of several individuals who were my personal spiritual professors was my client Deirdre Bounds, the founder of i-to-i, a gap-year travel company that she sold for in excess of $20 million. I was asked by her agent if I could help to raise Deirdre's profile in advance of the release of her book *Fulfilled*. I was a year into running my own PR business, having left the agency where I'd honed my craft. Deirdre's was a story of having suffered something of a life crisis. Lying face down in the mud in China, where she'd been teaching children to speak English, having toppled from her bicycle, drunk and incoherent, she met with her 'Checkpoint Charlie'. Vowing to change her life, she sought help for the alcoholism that was ruining her life. In embarking on the 12-Step program, she delved into the old resentments that lay beneath her pain. The result was the book *Fulfilled*, in which she shared the process she worked through to overcome her addiction, later launching her company and meeting her husband before starting a family. Needless to say, as her publicist, I had to read her book and work through the program as she'd done. It was my first introduction to the principles for living that underpin almost all spiritual teaching. Deirdre, without knowing, was one of my teachers.

I love the saying 'If all you ever do is all you have ever done, then all you will ever get is all you have ever got.' This next level of your life is going to require an evolved version of you and if you're to raise your game, you must raise your frequency. Frequency being that intangible level of consciousness, an energy that others feel before we even open our mouths. It's our vibe, our aura. The law of attraction tells us that we attract the same energy we emanate and quantum physics concurs that this isn't hippy fluff. We cannot con the universe, which is why the notion that we can 'fake it till we make it' is flawed. Faking anything is a recipe for disillusionment and short-term gain. You and I are here to play the long game – the ultimate game of life. But sweeping out the inner cobwebs that we all have is a necessary, if often uncomfortable, untrodden road to authentic power, peace and purpose.

We want to start operating on such a high frequency that as we walk into the room, the investor who has the purse strings to take our business idea from concept to creation feels the power of our intent. We want a frequency that compels customers through the authenticity of its communication. Building a brand or organization from a high-level frequency will always engage stakeholders, as communication from the heart has a power like no other. We are, after all, our own most powerful brand as the human being behind the project, business or role. If we aren't truly living the values we present to the world, then that conflict, that gap between truth and perception, is going to be the chink in our armour, which at some point will be our unravelling.

So what are your low-level habits? How we do anything is generally how we do everything and in pursuit of personal development for outer success, we need to get ruthless about the limiting habits that threaten to keep us stuck in a hamster wheel of repetition. One of my habits was quitting when I found myself in territory that took me beyond my natural areas of skill. Generating ideas has never been difficult for me. No visible multicultural greetings cards in the British high street? No problem! That's a mission I could manage. The limited supply of multicultural greetings cards in the USA and South Africa, the entire world, too? Sure, I could tackle a global multicultural greetings card deficit, too. And off I would go, horse bolting out of its cart, making it happen and revelling in the creative elements of starting a new business. Oh! the pleasure in conjuring up the imagery for the designs, the scrumptious joy of crafting the words for the captions... The fun of organizing the castings and photoshoots for the models... And my delight in the challenge of convincing narrow-minded retail buyers to step into the twenty-first-century marketplace and give up shelf place to sell my representative cards.

All this creative, communicative comfort-zone stuff was child's play for me, because it played to my strengths. Hell, I could even take on the New York Stationery Show seven months pregnant and alone, roller banner and stock in hand. And I could arrive at the Javits Center drenched from the rain and teary – where do the NY cabs disappear to in the rain? – and *still* seal a deal with Staples, one of America's largest chain stores.

But when it came to the 20-page contracts and spreadsheets, my eyes glazed over and my heart sank, for they required detail and a significant expansion of our offer to meet their criteria. Excel, figures and the finer details have never been my thing. Confession: I've spent my life creating grand plans, on which I embark with such vigour, enthusiasm and sheer energy that I've been able to convince most people to get on board with anything. Luckily, there have often been individuals to help connect the dots, so my big plans could be realized. In the case of this Staples deal, which might well have reaped huge commercial reward for the Color blind card range given the sheer gravitas of it being a multinational stockist, I did not. The buck stopped with me.

Confession part two: I *allowed* this deal to fall through under the pretence that I had 'too much on my plate'. It is indeed true that my plate did overflow-eth. I had a nine-month-old baby, a young teen daughter and was in the midst of a painful separation from my former partner. And all whilst trying to keep my PR business afloat, moving home and adjusting to our new reality. Emotionally I was wrecked. I felt like a failure for what I perceived as another failed relationship and I was physically exhausted. And yet the truth of it was that when I peeled back its blurred layers, none of these circumstances were the reason behind me not having pursued the Staples deal. The real truth is that I'm a gladiator and even with my life in the spin of a tornado, if I'd *truly* desired to fulfil the order that might have propelled my card range, then I could and would have done. I have slain greater dragons in my life, built a life from nothing on four hours' sleep, broke and baby in tow, so Staples was nothing.

The *truth* is that I came up against the yucky parts of business, which were beyond my zone of comfort, and so I fell back into my own excuses, bailing on my business and myself. It took me years to own that truth and actually admit that to myself, but in doing so I was able to learn a powerful lesson from the universe, meaning that if I'm smart, it won't ever happen again. Now, when I'm faced with columns and figures that seem to blur into meaningless bumf, leaving me wanting to dive straight into the closest creative task on my to-do list, I know that I have two options. Confront the task and digest the details in front of me slowly or seek help to gain clarity on the information at hand. Skirting around the necessary and bailing on the basis that I'm pushed beyond what's naturally comfortable for a left-brained wordsmith like me is no longer an option. I'm better than my BS.

What are your top three most limiting low-level habits? The habits that if you look closely, you'll see present at various junctures in your life. Same behaviour, just a different set of circumstances. We must weed these out and charge into them with a determination first to identify and then to exterminate, replacing them with action that takes us *towards* the greater version of ourselves and not away from it.

If tiptoeing around – or in the case of the Staples deal skipping town – when faced with spreadsheets is my practical limiting habit, seeking validation is one of my internal potholes. Needing the approval of others is one of the fastest ways to undermine your personal power and we live in a society powered by the desire of third-party endorsement. With all its brilliant possibilities, the digital world also introduced the marvel that is social media, a capability that quickly shifted from platforms offering the opportunity to connect with one another, to ones urging us to like, heart or follow one another as their central function. The more likes we secure, the better we feel, and without a strong and robust sense of self, it's easy to be swept up in judging our own worthiness on the basis of another's validation. I think it's no coincidence that today our teenagers in the West are suffering from higher levels of angst and depression than ever before. With an average four hours spent online each day, is it any wonder?

My personal need for validity from others is so entrenched that the moment I penned this part of the book and noted what I felt my own three limiting habits were, my immediate instinct was to call my husband for validation. He was sat peacefully at home watching the NBA basketball on television, minding his own business, yet I felt the urge to share them with him and ask whether or not he agreed these were indeed my leading bad habits! The irony wasn't lost on me.

These habits have lived in us for years and sometimes decades, so they're skilled at sneaking in when we least expect it! Having caught mine red-handed, I resisted the urge to call my husband to crosscheck with him, noted the power of my almost addictive urge to make the call, and made a silent pact not to read any more of my book to him until he requested it. I was happy to share my thoughts, for I loved the high-frequency conversations inspired by my latest chapter, which would have us speaking and reflecting into the early hours. But from that moment I was going to be certain that my need to share stemmed from a place of self-assured certainty and giving, rather than an ego-driven, needy, limiting prerequisite to hear how great (valid) it (I) was. Needing his or anybody's validation reinforces a deep-seated belief that we don't have the answers within us, that our own instincts and beliefs are somehow unreliable, that we cannot trust ourselves, that we aren't worthy – that we aren't enough. That great lie, which I believe is buried within many of us to varying degrees, is the untruth we're on a mission to expel.

It's incredible what we see when we slow down long enough to observe our own behaviour through the lens of excruciating truth. Once I started to dig, I could see clearly that my entire career had been an attempt to secure validation in society. I'd created my own self-importance. First through my high-powered jobs, working with famous people within a celebrity industry, feeding off 'fans' who perpetuate the false notion that any human being is somehow more valid than you or I. And then by lapping up the 'entrepreneur of the year' titles that were bestowed upon me, and through the high profile and validation that came with it. Seeking validity from anywhere outside of ourselves or on the basis of anything other than the values we live from and the contribution we make – who we are to the outside world rather than what we do for a living, what we look like or what we have – is completely meaningless and superficial. What's more, none of this will bring any of us *true* joy. Doing it for the likes rather than the love is a short-term plaster to a deep cut.

Limiting habits identified? Get vigilant for when those habits creep up and your thinking mind attempts to present a justification for them. Get militant on those bad boys, and stop at nothing to identify and exterminate them. It won't happen overnight, so be easy on yourself. The first step is in identifying them – the mastery will come with time.

Shed Your Skin

'In the struggle lies the joy.'
MAYA ANGELOU

Having the courage to confront your weaknesses and arrest your bad habits is to be celebrated. You're in the minority if you're someone who looks first at how they can resolve to change some aspect of their conditioning before apportioning blame elsewhere. There's a wholesome honesty about doing that which is badass – but yes, it's confrontational and often incredibly uncomfortable.

In this way, we have an awful lot in common with lobsters – those soft, squishy creatures that house themselves within their own hard shell. As lobsters grow, their shell becomes stifling, smothering and painful. Eventually, the lobster can bear it no longer, at which point it hides from predators under a rock, abandons its old shell and fashions a new one. This process happens again and again throughout the lobster's life, with its shells often looking completely different from the previous, so much so that the lobster in its new shell may be unrecognizable to its closest friends and even to itself.

Within this process of spiritual growth, the discomfort that can accompany the shedding of our old 'skin', whilst unquestionably the very thing that makes life open up to us and reveal its marvellousness, is not to be sniffed at. We're dealing with shifting the ways of being that have accompanied us for forever, overhauling our views and expectations about ourselves and our lives, inevitably choosing not to compromise on what we know deep down is true for us. Often, truth isn't the easy option and that conscious deliberate decision to speak when the room is silent, object when the masses are in unison, stand when your peers are seated, leave when the only certainty is in staying, is no gentle waltz. The comfort, though, is in knowing that forcing your growing anatomy to remain squished into a suffocating shell will result in the diminishing of your spirit. An unfulfilled, cosseted, squished lobster.

We can choose between a period of discomfort as we break free and transition from our old mould, or a lifetime of existing as a smaller version of all that we might become. Playing small, dimming our light, compromising on all of the magical possibilities just to exist in the ironically named 'comfort zone', is not comfortable, at all.

Don't be fooled by the masses who dwell in this space. Most people are unfulfilled. We live in a world where we've all anaesthetized our truth, hiding behind a representative with an airbrushed social media life, rather than being our true selves. There is disparity in our society, with growing political discord, an increase in mental health issues, a lack of housing and health-care provision, an anxiety epidemic in our children. We're more medicated than we ever have been before. What more evidence do we need to acknowledge that we're not OK! So why the hell are we all fronting and pretending to be? Pretence has become our norm. It's the normal thing to do to have surface-level, superficial interactions, where we mask who we truly are because the fear of rejection, of not being accepted, is intolerable. We all desperately want to belong, but miss the fact that true connection is only obtainable when we interact heart to heart.

Ultimately, every single one of us is faced with a choice. To live our truth or not to live our truth. I ponder on the question, but the reality is that the period of time when we had a choice in the matter is almost behind us. Everything that isn't real and authentic is eroding. We only need to watch the news to see real-world examples of how everything that isn't based on authenticity is imploding. There's a tide of change that's sweeping in, and as individuals, we find ourselves at a critical juncture. It is at this juncture that we can choose whether or not we ride the wave to an era where I believe our existence will be dominated by an elevated level of consciousness and true connectivity. Or we can drown in the tsunami of a world of materialism, separation and a way of being that's no longer sustainable.

Our collective spiritual evolution is inevitable and it's only the arrogance of a limited human mind that could fail to consider the possibility that human beings existing purely from body consciousness are the new pterodactyls. I don't think this – I know it to be true because I feel it. And I'm not alone. If you haven't yet heard of Rebecca Campbell, go and listen to *Rise Sister Rise*. I listened to much of her book with goose pimples punctuating my skin as this woman, the Australian former head of an advertising agency, spoke about the collective shift in consciousness as though she were reading my own heart. There's a growing itch, for some of you a mild irritation, for others a mosquito bite of a pang, but from independent souls to entire industries and countries, change and revolution is in the air. To ignore or deny it is to risk becoming a fossil.

Chatting to a girlfriend of mine, who is a director within the health service in London, currently prodding away at her own itch of a calling for more, we got to talking about Kanye West, as you do. What on earth has happened to Kanye?

This is an artist whose debut studio album *The College Dropout* earned him a Grammy for best rap album, on which he talked about materialism, religion, racism and higher education. This is a man who broke the mould in terms of the topics he broached. Whether you like his music or not, the man is an artistic genius who embodied what it is to embrace vulnerability as the birthplace of creativity. Globally, we lapped up his words from his rap 'All Falls Down', in which he displayed a distinct level of self-awareness, showing how material possessions boosted his self-esteem. The truth resonates. It sold over 4 million copies, being labelled by *Time Magazine* and *Rolling Stone* as 'One of the greatest albums of all time'.

Fast-forward 14 years and Kanye is reported to have been receiving support for mental health issues. None of his albums have impacted with the power of the first and this musical genius is most often seen from time to time in his wife Kim Kardashian's reality series. I make no judgement on either personality, beyond the observation that Kanye seems a high-profile example of the two conflicting facets that are common to all human existence – our conscious self and our egotistic self – the bit that thrives on validation from external sources. This is a man courageous enough to rap about God, when it was wealth and status that sold hit records, and admit the fact he couldn't go to the grocery store without being dressed up because he felt insecure. Yet, he's married into what is perhaps one of popular culture's most manufactured and contrived products. He's become a prop in his own movie scene, as immersed in fame and fandom as it is possible to be. But at what cost to his truth? We're all Kanye. All desperate to feel a part of and to belong. Yet, we're conditioned to believe we can attain this connection through what we have, what we do for a living and the influence of those we're associated with. It's the greatest lie.

Real connection is born out of stripping metaphorically naked and being who you are unapologetically. When we embrace vulnerability and allow ourselves to be truly seen, we empower others to disrobe, and it's from those honest interactions that unfurl all the connection the world is craving. Getting naked is where we truly get to meet each other and where we honestly get to meet our true selves. We've all got that Grammy award-winning album in us in some form. That talent that ignites our passion and lights up the world in a way that no other human being on Earth could replicate. That thing that's our God-given reason for being on this Earth. But to unleash such artistry regardless of our field, we have to step into vulnerability, forget all that we've been taught about who we *should* be and learn to express ourselves from our core.

So what are you resisting?

The first time I met Tracey I disliked her instantly. The class had been due to start at 1:35 p.m. and it was close to 1:45 p.m. when she entered the room without an apology to the room full of students ready to start. My mental smear campaign went into overdrive as I observed this young, attractive woman – she couldn't have been more than early thirties – who proceeded straight to the front of the class, commanding our attention instantly with a self-assured request that we assume our opening chant. *Surely* she should apologize? Aren't yoga teachers supposed to be about peace and love? I thought. Why doesn't she smile? Tracey was serious. She corrected our poses and issued directions with a firmness that irked me. I won't be coming to this class again, I thought, I didn't come here for this. She was no-nonsense and even a bit scary.

Tracey was my favourite teacher six months later and, if it's God's will, around the time this book hits the shelves I'll be in Goa at the Indian retreat she recommend I attend with her. I did go back, albeit accidentally, unaware of which teacher took each class at the time. What quickly became evident without her saying a word was that she was serious about yoga and about teaching it to the individuals who attended her classes. She was committed to the practice and she required, expected and encouraged the same level of commitment from us, both to the practice and to ourselves, just by being who she was.

There wasn't anything in particular she said that had an impact, it was simply who she was. Interesting that my instantaneous reaction, rejection even, of a person whose way of being wasn't in line with *my* idea of what a yoga teacher should be, was in actual fact the perfect individual to support me in my own exploration of myself – both on and off the mat. And support she did. Without fail, I left every class with a gem. 'This position isn't something to be got through, it's something to be experienced!' she would assert. How often in my life was I viewing the more challenging moments as hardships to be tolerated rather than felt and learned from? How many of us spend our lives living this way, missing the gems and learnings in every challenge?

Tracey not only taught yoga, she also challenged my preconceptions, forcing me to observe how I rejected that which was good and meant for me – just because it wasn't packaged as I felt it should be. Tracey was another catalyst to me becoming a bigger me and stepping into an opening that wasn't previously there. Who are the Traceys in your life? What are you rejecting or resisting that's uncomfortable, irritating, challenging, which, if you cease to resist, will reveal itself as a slip road towards a bigger you?

Get Lit

'Respond to every call that excites your spirit.'
RUMI

I reconvene with myself on my yoga mat. It's the space where, without distraction, I check in with myself. There's something celestial about a yoga mat. It can be the most unremarkable item, rather like a carpet without the magic, and then sometimes, just sometimes, it'll transport you.

My moment was in Shavasana. Back, head, legs to the ground, feet loosely falling open and palms to the sky, eyes closed at the end of a class, at which point I connected with other yoga-mat moments. They connected like a dot-to-dot, tracing back to a yoga session when the mat carried a body laden with pain, heavy with despair and fear. They couldn't cure Dad's cancer. Fast-forward to another moment and this time another studio, another mat, same body, same position, the mat upholding a body of sadness, tears rolling down cheeks to collect beside me on the mat. How would I, how could I...? And now, today, tears again, only this time they're of gratitude. I'm moved by my own peace – what beauty!

What a surprise to find serenity waiting on the other side of despair...

Perhaps the biggest challenge as I make my way along this trail without a destination, is in speaking this new language, seeing through this new lens and living this way of being, in a world that often still sees it as fluffy, naive or detached from reality. It's easy to meditate and emanate kindness in a conscious bubble, when we're in environments with like-minded people. But when everyday life sets in, falling back into our old reactive, judgemental and disconnected selves is an inevitability as we start down this road. The world for the most part doesn't think like this and a moral deficit prevails over our societies. It is this very conflict that forces us to confront the conflict within ourselves.

I fell in love with yoga around the same time my personal development journey kicked into fifth gear. A couple of my dearest friends, Ali and Jodie, were both long-time yogis and both were huge influences in encouraging me to try out what I perceived as a bit of a boring way to spend an hour relaxing. It's no coincidence that through my twenties I was a big-time 'body pump' fiend. I would spend an hour four times a week with 30kg (approx 65lbs) on my back, squatting, lunging and lifting weights to up-tempo, bass-pumping tracks, pushing my body to its limit, raising my heart rate and carving my body into its sleekest form. As I was in the gym, I was in life. I did everything to the max. 'More' was my mantra and while my ass looked good in jeans, my soul wasn't in good shape. Thanks to my girlfriends, my thirties brought yoga and neither my knees nor my spirit have desired to 'pump' ever since. In yoga I discovered a practice that brings us face to face with the complexity of our being. It's amazing and unquestionably it's an art which, along with writing this book and my husband's firm hugs, has been my own personal grief survival kit.

I've grown up on my yoga mat. It's inspired me to be gentler with myself as I've learned to refrain from forcing myself into positions that cause me strain. It's taught me about where I quit when the challenge becomes great. And the focus on my breathing is the space in which I've come to notice, and increasingly tame, my limiting thoughts and notions. All entirely transferable stuff that finds its way into life outside of the studio; I highly recommend it. And as I fall in love more deeply with this ancient art, which originated over 5,000 years ago, I think I might just find a retreat in India and explore this love affair more seriously. Dedicate some more of my life to it. Yoga and I might go steady. Not because I'm currently thinking of quitting my career to become a yoga teacher, but purely because it lights me up. And that, in my newfound romance with the now, is reason enough.

You are unfulfilled. You know your life is missing something and you're reading this book, so perhaps you've identified that 'something' to be purpose, but where to start in deciding your individual reason for being? The momentous question.

The answer is that you don't. And your job is to become OK with that for the time being. For today, our most pressing need is to reacquaint with ourselves with such intimacy that we begin to feed ourselves with the sustenance and fuel we need to light us up and carry us towards our truth. Our ultimate purpose born not out of the life we think we should be living or that the world expects us to live, but the one that leaves us dynamically awakened and soaring with the joy of being alive. That purpose that leaves no question as to whether or not we're doing what we're supposed to be doing. It feels good and right, and so it is.

Lose yourself so that time becomes meaningless, roles dissipate, expectations cease. Stripped back is where we meet ourselves.

As I child I danced. Ballet, tap, modern, jazz, all of it – four times a week for over a decade. I wasn't the best and nor was I the worst, but I adored it. Then I hit my teens and sourced my high elsewhere. Boys to make me feel wanted, work to make me feel valid and even weed for a period in my early twenties to dull the ache. When my son was away for a few days, without the need to dash back home from work for a story and bed, I signed up to a beginner's contemporary jazz class.

At first I hovered around the outskirts of the studio, close to the barre lest I might be seen, my body outed as an imposter, not having danced for so long. Until I noticed that almost everyone had the same look of self-consciousness written in their eyes. And as the music became louder, I edged further into the room and once again became lost in the dance. In dedicating an hour to an old joy, I reclaimed a lost love. As the class ended my eyes welled. Not with sadness, but with joyous release at reuniting with a long-lost friend, another piece of me. So many discoveries, insights and reclaimed memories have begun to flood back to me over the past year as though small, fragmented pieces of me have begun to return home and slot back together. And as I remember more of who I truly am, the parts of me that were left behind, I inhabit my body with greater ease and I own my space without apology.

As children, losing ourselves in the creativity of the moment comes naturally. We build tunnels and alternate worlds out of cardboard boxes, our hands become puppets, and we're allowed the freedom to explore outside of the constraints of routine and responsibility. Then we grow up, and the education system and often our parents begin to coerce us into a series of fear-based decisions about how we'll spend a significant portion of our precious years on this Earth. What's happening in the job market? How will we get on to the property ladder? How can we achieve job security? Where are the opportunities? These questions are well intentioned but fail to consider or even identify the existence of personal inclination, desire, passion or purpose. Years later, when we've slathered on layers of existence in order to tick the right boxes, we emerge somewhere on the scale between unfulfilled, depressed and sick, questioning what life is all about and thinking there has to be more than this! Meanwhile, beneath the layers, our true calling waits to be rediscovered and unleashed...

A friend of mine called Jessica Ashby could have been a professional figure skater. From the age of 10 until she was almost 18, each morning she trained for several hours while her classmates slept, before beginning her school day. Competing in numerous contests, including the British championships, she'd always expected to pursue the sport in which she was so naturally talented, once she finished school. However, with the after-effects of puberty kicking in around the age of 16, Jessica's commitment to her social life began to rival her dedication to figure skating. With her child's body developing into that of a woman, she needed to train ten times as hard in order to realize the same results. With the appeal of having fun with her friends beginning to supersede her desire to skate, at 18 she quit the sport altogether.

Studying media at university was, admits Jessica, the easy option. Her parents owned an entertainment media company and so, on graduation, she took up a seat at the picture desk of the family business for most of her twenties in a role and industry that was neither inspiring nor challenging for her. It was just a job, for which she had very little ambition.

'I disliked a lot about the media industry. I found it contrived, patronizing and for the most part just wrong.' A close friend of the late legend Amy Winehouse, Jessica admits that often she would visit to find paparazzi waiting outside to photograph her vulnerable friend. Feeling incredibly compromised, her conscience pricked, she knew she had to get out.

Deciding to make use of her knowledge of the media industry in a more positive way, she decided to retrain as a media teacher, applying for one of the UK's most respected and coveted universities, narrowly missing out on a place. Around the same time an old skating friend got in touch to say that a contact was looking for someone to join a circus and tour around Spain for three months. Jessica had only skated sporadically for fun since walking away from the sport 10 years prior, but admits, 'Something inside me thought I really, really want to do this!' She impulsively signed up, but then fear set in and she dropped out just days before she was set to leave the country.

'I got cold feet. I didn't want to leave my family, didn't want to leave the country. Something just didn't feel right about going, so reluctantly I let my friend down last minute.'

A couple of days later, sitting miserably at the desk of the media agency she was desperate to leave, Jessica received a call from the university stating that a dropout meant a place had become available on the teacher training course she was desperate to take. The universe was doing its thing.

'The course woke me up. It was one of the best years of my adult life as I was so invested in what I was learning,' admits Jessica. On graduating she got a job quickly and began teaching secondary school pupils, experiencing phenomenal results through her genuine desire to see them thrive. She fell in love with teaching, but found herself at odds with an educational institution that focused more on end-of-term grades that boosted the school's rating than actually nurturing the individual passion and natural talent of its students. Then four years after her teaching career had begun, Jessica found herself discussing career options with the tutor group who'd started school around the same time Jessica had begun teaching.

'They were exploring their next steps and future career options, and as I told them to follow their passion, it sparked a question in me as to whether or not I was following my own advice. While I loved working with the students, on some level I knew that teaching within an institution whose values weren't congruent with my own wasn't where I was supposed to be.'

A friend had invited Jessica to an evening pole-dancing class months earlier and she'd quickly become a natural. Her muscle memory from her skating days kicked in, reigniting her love of performance. The enjoyment inspired her to think about circus as another hobby she could explore and having randomly found a circus school via Google, a love affair ensued with the art that sees acrobats spin through the air.

'I'd sit at my desk listening to music, fantasizing about routines I could perform, with mood boards of trapeze pin-up girls decorating my desk. Certain pieces of music just moved me and it took me back to when I was a child skating.'

The itch wouldn't go away. There was a full-time course at the circus school where she was already training in the evenings, which required a substantial financial investment. Beyond that, now in a serious relationship with her partner and committed to a mortgage, Jessica couldn't see how it would be possible for her to pursue her newfound passion and still make her loose five-year plan of having a child a reality. Thankfully, her partner saw differently and persuaded her that a career pivot was entirely possible with his support, encouraging her to sign up.

'Within weeks I handed in my notice, quit in the summer and started a full-time course in circus arts in the September. It was like falling in love for the first time. Every ounce of me was where I wanted to be and part of the exhilaration was that there was no end goal. Once the course finished I knew that what happened next was whatever I made of the opportunity.'

Today, Jessica earns a stable living as a physical performer, merging both her skating and circus talents, as well as teaching aerial and wellness classes.

'The best part is knowing that I made it all happen myself. I took the most inspiring parts of my life and brought them all together to create a working world that's unique to me. I can't really call it a job, because it's what I want to be doing, what I'm meant to be doing. And I'm doing it authentically, because I believe in it. And I believe in my ability to create the life I want for myself.'

When I last spoke to her she was breastfeeding her eight-month-old son having just completed a rehearsal for her forthcoming show in aid of World Mental Health Day in a couple of months.

'Everything I've ever done has led to this moment. This moment in your life is not the be all and end all – you can always change direction. If you really believe in what you want to do, you will always find a way to make it work.'

True liberation is the state of completeness that comes with releasing the craving to be significant in the eyes of others. You're the only audience that matters and your obligation to yourself is to make your life an unforgettable masterpiece of a show without regrets. Who or where you were yesterday is inconsequential to this present moment, in which you can choose to live your life deliberately and courageously. No permission required.

Choose Happy

*'There is no such thing as good weather,
or bad weather. There's just weather
and your attitude toward it.'*
LOUISE HAY

When we no longer need to be admired, acknowledged or deemed significant by others it is freeing. Not caring what others think is liberating – but releasing yourself from the grip of your own stale internal thought patterns is revelatory.

I loved the HSBC Bank ads the moment I first noticed them in the tunnel where you wait to board the plane at the airport. If you haven't seen them, they depict two different images with words beneath. For example, it might be a man in a suit with a stiff demeanour with the word 'Leader' beneath and another more relaxed guy in jeans with the word 'Follower'. There's another in the series showing three images of a cow, beneath which are the words 'Dinner', 'Deity' and 'Leather', suggesting that how we view the images is entirely down to our personal perception and our values. We don't all see the same thing. In fact, more than that, what we see isn't actually real at all. How we view everything is based purely on the experiences that inform our personal outlook. Which is just great. Because digesting this revelation changes life in all sorts of ways.

What this means is that if our interpretation of any given event or thought about a situation leaves us feeling depleted, we can notice how it makes us feel and instead opt for a neutral, unloaded thought about the matter. That pause and space is critical, where we weigh up the validity of the thought that's leaving us feeling 'less than'. This is because it allows us time to look closer at whether the cow we're perceiving as leather really *is* leather or whether our shoe obsession is blurring our judgement. Has she really not responded to your email because she isn't interested in working with you on the project, or did it simply go into your spam folder?

I've been a prize-winning negative overthinker for ages. I used to come up with entire mental essays around why my emails weren't returned, why he hadn't called, why she didn't 'like' my post, why that client didn't come on board, why he slept with his back to me... At the end of my analysis on all of these counts my final conclusion was generally that it was because I was shit. That pesky belief of not being enough leaked its way into every facet of my life like the rotten tomato that infects the other fruit in the bowl, and my goodness it was exhausting.

We all tend to play out the same tired outlook in all areas of our lives. The only difference is that while my underlying point of view might be 'I'm not good enough,' yours might be

'Do you love me?' The point of view will change somewhat, but it's always a fear-based perspective that lies beneath the surface of our consciousness, because that's how society and life in an unconscious world wires us. That's the outlook jail we're escaping.

Rewinding to five or so years ago, my baby boy was the most angelic ray of sunshine. He never cried, he slept well through the night after just a few months and he smiled endlessly. The joy he brought was infinite. Then around the age of two he seemed to transform into a cross between a gremlin and Road Runner. My former angel developed a penchant for screeching his discontent, actually physically screaming, and a talent for highly skilled bedtime acrobatics. This meant that the bars of his cot were no test for a baby who didn't approve of lights out. By 18 months, my son was catapulting himself out of his cot by scaling the rungs and flinging his toddler legs up and over the sides, landing with a thud, two feet on the ground, then racing into the living room where I'd be expecting him.

Though this nightly routine that went on for several weeks was exhausting, since it meant the whole bedtime routine could last several hours as I redeposited him in his cot before he Spider-manned his way out again, it was remarkable nonetheless. His steely determination and stubbornness was evident early on. And as his speech developed, this desire to debate my parenting skills and dictate his own rules became verbalized. He questioned everything and objected to most things, with tantrums ensuing when his will – 'let's paint a beautiful butterfly on the living-room wall!' – wasn't granted.

I couldn't understand how parenting second time around felt so much more challenging. What on earth was I doing wrong?!

Then one day, as I lamented how difficult my otherwise scrumptious boy had become, a girlfriend stopped me in my tracks. 'Maybe your son's just exceptional?' And in that moment everything changed. My mindset and outlook shifted. My son was indeed intuitive and questioning, and he had this beautiful empathy for others, which had a maturity beyond the levels of compassion of most adults. He'd make 'old soul' remarks that suggested he'd lived many lives before and was unswervingly unique. From that one statement, the way I viewed my son and his behaviours shifted completely. I met him where he was, and in embracing his individuality and adjusting my attitude, his behaviour followed suit.

Accepting him for who he was, I began to factor in more time to devote to the discussion that I knew was inevitable before going anywhere or doing anything, rather than constantly attempting to rein him in to my fixed views and ways of doing things. I became flexible, allowing him to manoeuvre and explore, still creating boundaries but also giving my wonder boy the space to express himself. As a result of the change in how I received him, the wayward elements of his personality lessened, as he had nothing to resist. Our bond has deepened and at six years old, I see him as the incredible, unique being that he is. I adore his exploratory and questioning traits, and I let him flow – even if it does take an hour longer to get dressed in the morning.

On so many levels, perspective is a superpower of a gear shift. Imagine applying the perspective shift to your difficult boss or co-worker, or that business plan you've been putting off writing? We can seek the light in everything and the joy is that when it's the light we're looking for, that's exactly what we find.

Identifying the source of where my sense of lack stemmed from – and devoting some attention to loving the little girl in me who decided somewhere 30 years ago that she was the reason Dad shouted and Mum left – was a pivotal moment in being able to handle the tiniest of perceived rejections with neutrality, without making them all confirmation of my insufficiency. The point is that there are always multiple perspectives on absolutely everything. Pausing before you commit to yours and opting for the perspective that points in the direction of your best self is where mastery begins. All of our thoughts either stem from fear or love, explains spiritual teacher Marianne Williamson. So once you accept the idea that just because you think it, it doesn't make it factual, it becomes easier to discard the low-vibe thoughts you'd once have entertained and instead opt for a more neutral perspective.

Life always gives us every misfortune, every red light, every obnoxious supervisor or employee, every divorce and every bankruptcy. Every lesson that we need to learn is presented to us in the form of a challenge ready for us to step up to. The norm is to lament over everything from the weather to our financial situation or health troubles. But while having a good moan might bring some momentary satisfaction – particularly when shared with a moaner friend – it's a sort of McDonald's cheeseburger feel-good. Pleasurable in the moment but violating afterwards. Each time we complain, we disempower ourselves by focusing on all that isn't as we'd like it to be. That focus means that not only do we leave ourselves feeling small and victims of circumstance, but we also attract more circumstances that reinforce dissatisfaction in our lives.

A couple of years ago one of my besties, the actress Ali Bastian, who is like a human fairy light, such is the warmth and lightness of her vibe, had just returned from Bali and was raving about a book called *A Complaint Free World*. The book told of a minister in Missouri, America. He'd appeared on *Oprah* and had sold more than 11 million 'non complaining' bracelets in 106 countries globally. Quite the phenomenon. Having finished the book, she gave me her copy along with a band, and I got stuck in.

The first revelation was 'Oh my goodness! I had no idea I complained so much.' The challenge is to wear a purple plastic bracelet on your wrist for 30 days without complaining once and watch your life transform. Except that if you complain even once, you switch your bracelet to your other hand and you have to start again at day one. It took me 10 days to complete one full day without complaining! The honest truth is that I didn't get to 30 days because I became distracted and forgot to maintain the level of self-monitoring required to keep my positive outlook up. What happened within less than a week, however, was remarkable. For me, it was one of the most powerful living examples of the fact that whatever we focus on, we attract more of.

Having become aware that like most human beings I found multiple things to moan about before I'd even left the house,

I began to bite my lip when my daughter didn't drink the smoothie I'd prepared, the meeting was cancelled, I burned my top whilst ironing, whatever. The more I bit my lip and resisted the urge to vocalize my complaint, the more I found the people I interacted with were happier and more chilled. Because *they* were happier, they gave me less reason to be narked. And my relationships with everybody around me, both in and outside of the office, improved – even though I was the only one doing the non-complaining challenge.

My husband, who was my boyfriend at that point, who usually paid little attention to my latest personal development process, was so weirded out by my new light demeanour and how much calmer I'd become, that he hit Amazon and ordered his own copy. Suddenly, we were two people in one household not complaining. The impact of this on us as individuals, not to mention on our home, was incredible. An outsider would have thought we'd had some other huge upturn in our circumstances, but all of the practical challenges remained – it was us who were choosing to respond to them differently. We weren't pretending challenging stuff wasn't happening, but because we were consciously opting not to reinforce the problem by grouching about it, we were left with the space to be solution-oriented and had a less stressed-out temperament, making the challenges easier to manage.

In the pause, we were able to consider higher thoughts of alternative ways to perceive everything from illness to parking tickets. Life got better professionally, as well. I related better to my staff and actually ordered copies for them all. The entire process was illuminating, as within your own newfound self-awareness and light energy, you become much more conscious of the energy frequency of the people around you. You can suddenly see clearly why some people seem to go through life fighting one battle after another and experiencing a stream of endless problems. With my new more peaceful disposition, I was a better leader for my team, which meant they responded positively and were more effective in their roles, which was great for business. Every phone conversation and email I sent went out with an energy of positivity and lightness, and so I received positivity and flow back from the universe. This stuff works!

As I made changes within myself, the world around me changed to meet me at my new higher frequency. And I still find the mere fact that we have such tremendous capacity to impact our worlds, out of this world. It blasts into the gutter the notion that we're all here as victims of whatever life throws at us, moving us from a mindset of victimhood to empowerment. We can all change the world and I believe this of everything, but it starts with changing ourselves and as we do so, the domino effect of impacting our families, our communities and beyond becomes possible. Powerless limpets we are not. We just need to show up for the challenge of overhauling our old, tired ways of being.

As what came out of my mouth began to change, so did my thoughts. The space in which I usually said, 'I'm tired', or 'this client is doing my head in,' was replaced with a gap that allowed me to consider why I wasn't prioritizing sleep and taking control of my routine. It also allowed me to pause and look at whether the clients I was representing at that time were the ones I *wanted* to work with – and then I could make a call on what needed to change. Sometimes, the pause simply bought me a moment to remember that I choose my life the way it is because I choose my life the way it is! In that simple mental note to myself, I was empowered rather than disempowered by my circumstances.

Not complaining is a bit like jumping off a runaway train. When we become aware, we end the jail sentence of being a prisoner to our wild thoughts, many of which are programmed to be fuelled irresistibly by fear, blame and negativity stored from old baggage. In my case, this has meant regularly confronting my inner saboteur, who questioned my ability to make a success of my professional life and even to make my marriage work because of a false notion that I'm not enough. When we master our words, mastering our thoughts follows suit and from that place, life gets jiggy.

As I write this I'm transported back to the period where my hubby and I were two wristband-wearing happy people surfing over tribulation, wondering why we stopped. Probably because we got distracted by life and slipped back into that comfortable magnetic thing called old habits. Non-complaining, like gratitude, is an art to be practised, a craft to be developed, and the only way we can ingrain it in our life toolkit is to dedicate to it consistently. Today, keeping my gratitude list, a simple list of all the things that have brought me joy during the day, is a nightly ritual. Though it's a simple step involving just a few minutes of focus, a piece of paper and a pen, when I fall off the wagon and stop reminding myself of all of the small but joyous happenings and observations in my life, I inevitably slip back into my default setting of lack. Lack is the quagmire where something is always wrong, where it's all too good to be true. It's the fertile soil where my insecurities and saboteur can erupt, and it's a slippery slope into the vortex of depression which I know well. So for me, the gratitude list and a commitment to choosing my words with consideration are holy.

A few months after my dad passed on, I decided to begin hosting monthly dinner parties at our home, where we'd invite 10 guests who hadn't met each other before, to connect, chat and laugh. Now to give this some context, you have to understand that I'm no natural-born chef. If it weren't for the fact that my parents and their home-cooked meals were around the corner, my poor daughter would've been raised on three meals in rotation – Nigella Lawson I am not. In the last couple of years however, burnout from 15 years of relentless graft forced me to reassess my life balance and so with a little more time to play, post age 35 I learned to cook properly.

The dinner parties gave me the opportunity to exercise my cooking skills on a large-ish group for the first time. I found that I loved hosting and the day of prep, with Sade blasting from the speaker, was a joy in itself. Some nights we'd play games and drink copious amounts of wine. Other nights the conversation would turn to politics and inequality, where we'd move around the table sharing our greatest triumph and challenge of the week. We even had a random listening session of a music artist friend's new album. Our friends always brought a bottle or a bunch of flowers to thank us, but honestly we got so much more from their presence in our home. For the first time in forever, I'm now socializing consistently in a way that lights me up and I swear that laughter is the best therapy of all.

The benefit of getting deliberate about fixing the lack of social time and friendship in my life spills out from the Friday nights into smiling Saturdays and fulfilled Monday mornings. I'm a happier, better me because of my dinner parties and for that reason alone, it's a non-negotiable diary date along with yoga for life, my six-year-old's drawings on the walls, scented candles and flowers ever present in my home. Revere how the little things help to make the happiest of lives.

Embrace Visibility

*'Perhaps we should love ourselves so
fiercely that when others see us they
know exactly how it should be done.'*
RUDY FRANCISCO

M y personal development has been a bit like a testing jigsaw puzzle. I started off with a table full of separate pieces and took years to find the first two that slotted together. As I fixed one into the next I found another right under my nose and a momentum built up, until the correct missing piece was right before my eyes, slotting easily into the growing picture. Over the last year, more buried memories of my entire 37 years have floated to the surface of my mind than in my entire life. It's as though through the writing of this very book dots have begun to connect and suddenly I can see clearly how everything that I've ever done has led to me being in this precise moment.

As a lost teen just before I became pregnant with my daughter, I was washing hair in a local West London salon. I had no desire to be a hairdresser, but had dropped out of college intent on earning my own money so that I might have independence from my family. My parents were dismayed, but home life was tough and I'd already figured that fast-tracking to adulthood was going to be my best shot at a peaceful life. As a junior in the salon we had to make small talk with the clients, and on one particular day I began speaking to an immaculately dressed customer while managing to avoid splashing water over her face. She noted my intelligence and said that I shouldn't be washing hair, instead inviting me to her office in Holland Park, London.

Figuring that an office job had to be better than sweeping hair and cleaning skirting boards, I rocked up to her office the following week, where I was shown how to answer the phone. 'Connie Filippello Publicity, how can I help?' was the greeting... My first day as an office junior for the publicist to Mariah Carey and George Michael had begun, and my magical break into the media, which I would later return to as a young, desperately ambitious mum, had presented itself.

Just a handful of years after that chance salon meeting I found myself sitting beside Mariah Carey by candlelight. It was 3 a.m. in a swish New York loft recording studio, and I was one of several journalists who'd been flown to Manhattan, New York, at the expense of the record label, to interview Mariah for various publication cover stories. I wasn't yet 25 and this was a major coup for *Pride Magazine*, the women's glossy I was now working for as a senior writer. Connie herself requested I conduct the interview. From a chance chat over a washbasin, to a pivotal door opening to my career in media, all because I said *yes* – without a clue as to what was to come. If I hadn't accepted Connie's invitation to her office, I might never have discovered what public relations was, let alone have secured a job and later have crafted a great living from PR. I thought I was just going to upgrade my job so that I could stop sweeping up hair – I never could have predicted that I was about to walk through a doorway into my career for the next 20 years.

We never know that the net is going to appear before we leap. That would be too easy and far too safe. If we knew that every jump would result in us being caught, then ours would be a world of individuals soaring into the sky. But we don't and so only the courageous prepared to step off the ledge ever get to experience the magic that happens midair. Turning us from people who play small and stick to safe territory, to real life explorers constantly pushing back the boundaries of our own lives to reveal a little more of life's secrets.

I believe there's a divine plan for all of us. We're all talented, special and entirely unique, and there's a precise reason we're all on the Earth – to light it up with our purpose. Whatever you do, embrace the moment the universe invites you to step forwards and take your place. Say yes. Embrace the unknown!

A huge part of the reason I love my role as someone who supports women in stepping into their calling, is because of this wondrous ability to create visibility for the individuals I coach. From the mum making a living from her kitchen to the corporation investing half a million pounds into up-skilling disadvantaged kids with tech capabilities, it's a tool that lets the world know what these individuals and businesses are up to. This spotlight has incredible potential to help the people I work with become bigger versions of themselves by reaching new audiences, garnering support and basically blasting them into public consciousness. The most exciting element of the visibility that harnessing both traditional and social media creates, is all the unknown opportunities and possibilities that present themselves when you become visible. An incredible convergence happens when you share your message or brand with the world from an authentic space. Your tribe finds you. Your people. Those who believe the same things that you believe and who care about the things you care about. They spot you, and will support and get behind you and your mission. As Marianne Williamson says, 'There is nothing enlightened about shrinking so that other people won't feel insecure around you.' If you're lurking side of stage, ask yourself why.

It was an article in a national newspaper reporting I was the winner of an Enterprise Award alongside a photograph of me with the prime minister that caught the eye of America's biggest greetings card distributor. They went on to sell our Color blind cards in the USA – before we'd even begun to think about selling internationally. Just this one newspaper article led to me becoming a global exporter.

And it was a YouTube clip of me delivering a rambling but heartfelt speech to a conference room of female entrepreneurs that inspired a man I'd met once to make contact to tell me of his admiration – we were married five years later.

My entire life has been a series of 'yeses' that have opened up new and wonderful professional and personal adventures that I could never have predicted. Yes, there's a risk of getting injured on the pitch or even losing the game. Perhaps you'll even miss the crucial shot and feel humiliation. But there's no gain at all to be had sitting in the wings for fear of what might happen if you step out. No opportunity to improve your game, no chance of having your talent spotted. Nothing but the promise of regret as you question whether or not today was the day you might have scored that legendary goal.

A couple of years back on New Year's Eve a group of friends and I got together to celebrate. Just before midnight we sat around and discussed the one main goal we all wanted to achieve in the coming year. My bestie, Nana, publicly promised that the coming year would be the year she finally passed her driving test and got on the road. A mum in business with two kids, she needed the independence and had been reliant on her husband for transport for far too long.

For some reason driving was Nana's 'thing' – we all have it. That thing we put off and procrastinate over for so long that it grows horns and becomes an ominous, almost insurmountable challenge in our own mind. We all decided to make Nana accountable by donating £10 each towards her driving lessons – not because she needed the cash, but because we wanted her to commit.

A few months ago, I got a call from her to say that not only had she passed her test, but she had also bought her first car. Since then she's lit up the stars with her capacity to create. Each time she says *yes* to an opportunity, the universe responds with more abundance. From taking her

Love Yaa Yaa brand to New Orleans to sell at the Essence Festival, to going to Paris for the Afro Punk Festival, where she was scouted for her creative prowess, she was promptly offered a pop-up shop in a top Parisian boutique hotel. In the past year I've witnessed her travel, thrive and truly live. Today, alongside running her business, she's an advocate for Etsy, the multimillion-pound online marketplace. And just last week she was at Parliament in London to lobby for better support for microbusiness owners. She conquered her driving fear and the entire universe opened up to her.

I'm so inspired by this woman who I love so much, because there's a lesson here for all of us about what happens when we unshackle ourselves. When we tackle our 'thing' – or more often 'things' – our onerous limiting beliefs, to reveal the beauty in who we become on the other side. I'm so excited watching her adventure unfold.

Everything rolls out in our lives as it is meant to be. There are consequences when we fail to embrace the opportunities presented to us by the source that shows up in the form of genius ideas that strike whilst we're bathing the kids, when we're having a conversation with a friend in which she suggests a book we should read, or when we're invited to an event but flake last minute to watch TV. Each time we say no to the signpost that presents itself, we say no to life, working against the natural plan that's unfolding for us. There are no coincidences. Say yes to pursuing those genius ideas when they occur. Read the book. Attend the event. Let your life be one big unfolding adventure of learning, inspiration and exploration. And trust that even if it doesn't work out, you'll have taken some gem simply from the act of entertaining an enquiring mind.

Step into visibility rather than being held back by the fear of whether or not others will like or approve of what you say or do. Know that you're not for everybody and not everybody is for you – and that's OK. You only need to do you in all your individual glory, and *your* people will feel your values and find you. The whole idea of a constructed personal brand is outdated. *You* are your personal brand, and everything you believe, say and do is a manifestation of this brand. What is the vision of the person you intend to become? If today is your 'before' shot, then what does your 'after' look like? I'm not talking about aesthetics – I'm talking about your way of being.

Whilst my temptation may always be to compare the shortcomings of who I am today with my vision for the woman I intend to grow into, if I step back and observe my personal growth over the years there's no question that I love who I'm becoming. Do you like who you're becoming? What are the areas of yourself that you need to address? What limiting beliefs are you committed to quashing? What qualities are you keen to develop? What skill will you equip yourself with this year? Who is it time to forgive? Our personal brand will be a lifelong evolution and it doesn't require perfection. Right now, today, you're exactly where you're meant to be.

As I write this, I'm battling with my ultimate mental monster; that Scrooge who's determined to see me miss my deadline for submitting this book. That brute who's going all out – nine days before I'm due to complete this project – to convince me that this book is rubbish. That I'm rubbish and that I should give up. My heart has been so heavy and my mind so murky in the last few days that last week my inner critic gave me a panic attack and I had to leave a concert I was attending. I fled to my bed, so bogged down with negative mental noise that I literally couldn't remain in my seat at that moment.

This is where I am. I get close to greatness and my saboteur comes out, swagger turned up full blast to box me into submission. But I'm writing through it. Breathing and just letting the words spill out as my defence. Each time I think I've sparked out my demons, another presents itself for tackling. My vision for myself is one of getting to a place where I quit questioning my worth or validity. Knowing, without doubt, that I'm enough. But this is where I am today, perfectly imperfect and a little more serene, a little more self-assured with each new day.

I know I'm not alone with this perfection habit. This belief that until we're 100 per cent the finished article we mustn't step out and be seen. Newsflash: the very parts of you that you've been seeking to suppress or disguise are the parts of you that will often be the very thing that makes you shine. Trying to fit in and morph into other people's mould won't work, because people feel inauthenticity even if they can't put their finger on exactly what it is that doesn't ring true. We can only be truly authentic when we're the same person in all areas of our lives. The same person who rocks up to the office and sits in front of clients, the same person who chats to the family over dinner, the same person sandwiched into the morning commute around strangers. When we truly become who we are, we become a vibrational match for all that we want to attract and all that we want to become. This is the basic premise of the law of attraction and if you understand it, you'll know it to be true.

The law of attraction is also why we can often feel like frauds. We flit between roles and ways of being to fit in and conform to the environment we find ourselves in, afraid of not being accepted. But if we aren't allowed to be who we are in any given space – be it our relationship, our place of work or otherwise – then it means we don't belong there. When you're courageous enough to accept that the need to be real is more pressing than the need to fit in, you'll find that your people are attracted to you magnetically, your crew will find you. But you have to disrobe first so that they'll recognize you.

I was 12 years old when I stumbled upon the superficiality of belonging. Fitting in is a mirage. It's made of sawdust, without substance and as impermanent as a blow-dry in the rain. Fitting then that it was my hair that pleased me – a dark brown shoulder-length frizz, which for as long as I had been old enough to 'style' it myself had been worn with an unfashionable range of bands and bows. My sense of style was somewhat unique. I was a child whose idols had been the fictional characters of ballet. Giselle, Coppélia the doll, the err... swan in *Swan Lake*. I'd been in love with ballet and the release that I found in both the music and the movement from about the age of five.

On arrival at secondary school, I discovered that my pirouette wasn't cool. I also quickly found that my frizzy up-dos and bows were at odds with the gelled-back styles and slick curls that the other girls of mixed heritage seemed to rock so self-assuredly.

I recall one particular 'own clothes day', when we were encouraged to leave our uniforms at home. It turned out a small crowd was assembled at the front gates apparently awaiting my arrival to view my ensemble. I felt good in my oversized 'Say no to drugs and yes to life!' T-shirt – a souvenir of a past charity show dance I'd performed in – worn underneath a ballet belt and polished with a large piece of fluorescent pink net in my frizzy bouffant. I might even have been wearing jazz shoes. To me, I looked great in the mirror that morning. I really felt ready to take on the world in my random-yet-inexplicably-me outfit.

Yet, by 9:05 a.m. that morning my confidence had evaporated and I'd never felt more uncomfortably dressed. It wasn't just that my look was at odds with the uniform of expensive trainers, jeans, branded sweaters and glossy hair, but for the first time I also reconsidered all that I deemed appropriate about the way I presented my aesthetic to the world. Aged 12, I decided that being who I was didn't enable me to fit or belong.

Nana Fosu – a black girl of Ghanaian heritage with a smart brain, sharp tongue, and ability to attract friends and followers just by being her – was cool. Nana was late to school every day. What's more, though she always missed the school bell, I never once saw her run or even jog the 10-minute walk from the station. It was as though detention and reprimand were meaningless to this force of a girl who called her own shots and dictated her own start time. And while my punctuality was dictated by a dad who insisted on dropping me off in his car each morning – even when this became a great cause for embarrassment in my teens – on some level we were similar souls, both committed deeply to our own way of doing things and rebels to conformity.

I resisted the pack mentality for some time. But in a school environment where peer group exclusion is the ultimate stigma, before the first term had ended I'd cast my extensive collection of berets and hair netting into the trash, succumbing to an aesthetic overhaul. One afternoon in the girls' toilets Nana, with her magical, cool hands, sprayed a bottle of L'Oréal wonder into my long, dark and wild frizz. When I glanced up into the mirror Jessica, the aspiring ballerina, had transformed into a Jesika of glossy ringlets. Sandra D had become *Grease*'s Sandy. A girl on trend with the current hairstyles, who was cast admiring looks through the school gates by boys from neighbouring schools. A 12-year-old who'd never be seen dead in jazz shoes outside of a dance studio, who soon after hung up her ballet shoes once and for all.

That afternoon I reinvented myself with Nana's help, oblivious to the fact that young Nana, seemingly confident and cool, was immersed in her own battle of identity and belonging. She was a dark-skinned girl navigating puberty and attempting to fit in in a society where fair skin was deemed as the aesthetic of beauty.

Today, oh today, please label me anything but conformist. For each day, as I grow a little more into who I originally was and retrace sacred steps back to who I am, my footsteps grow more bold and more definite. With each day of being me, I become a little more liberated and certain. And though in some environments I step farther away from fitting in with the crowd, I find a sense of belonging in my own soul. There in the warm embrace of truth, both loneliness and exclusion cease to exist.

It's the world, not our hair nets or jazz shoes, which is weird. We walk around interacting with each other from behind masks. I introduce you to my swanky job title and you introduce me to the letters after your name. You present me with your bank balance and I respond with my list of awards. You show up with your résumé and I introduce you to my social media following. And so we interact and communicate on the basis of sawdust. Fluff. Which has everything to do with what we have and nothing to do with who we are.

Living in and subscribing to the values of that false world, it's impossible not to feel compelled to compare ourselves to our peers and draw comparisons that bring out the most negative of human attributes: fear, resentment, jealousy and feelings of insufficiency, which drive this insatiable desire for more. More wealth, more power, more stuff. A better body, a better house, a better job. And from that space, where the false notion that happiness can be attained through the acquisition of more materially, utter dissatisfaction at the least and war at the most are the result.

But there is another way. For in knowing that the truth of who we are has nothing to do with anything as superficial as our worldly items and accomplishments, we can introduce one another to who we truly are and what we care about. When I can venture into that sacred realm of vulnerability to say, 'Hello, nice to meet you – here's a glimpse into me,' you're then given permission to let me see you honestly. From that holy space of truth, the interactions and relationships that are built are of substance. Imagine the deals that could be brokered and the change that could be implemented if we conducted business from that fertile ground of integrity... Imagine if our world leaders were able to override the fear of losing their power to the opposition for long enough to reveal themselves, and to be the pure love that was and can again be – our natural state.

We live in a world in which the divides and threats of walls risk leaving it a place where we're shoehorned into clinging to cliques based on politics, race and socioeconomics. Those ideals we can opt into for safety in numbers. But most beautiful of all is that beneath the fickle mirage of circumstance, status, ethnicity and gender, we're all the same. One and the same – a manifestation of source love.

In loving relationships, the most rewarding partnerships are those in which two people become vulnerable and 'fall in love', overriding the fear of rejection or disappointment in order to enjoy a feeling of connection with another person. Our day-to-day interactions aren't so dissimilar. While we might not feel a compelling desire or attraction for the individuals we work with or pass on the daily trip into the office, if we viewed our fellow people without this default setting of judgement and suspicion, we'd awaken an opportunity to truly meet each other. Separation and difference are a lie. Our human need to belong to cliques is a symptom of our disconnection from our truth. The only medicine then is a return to that truth, a return to being who we are, once again becoming love.

Trust that the universe has a plan for you. Your most pressing duty is to become more of you, day by day doing what's required to make your thoughts, words and actions align into synchronicity. And as you begin to reach that space, life will start to flow. Outside of it, life is a struggle, because all the things in your life that don't correlate with your truth will feel increasingly hard to hold on to. It can be a tough pill to swallow, but let your faith become strong, so that you can do what's required to become who you truly are.

Every day that we step out into the world, it's 'own clothes day' and the world is waiting to see your outfit. Rock your frizzy hair and jazz shoes with pride. Be the change. Be love.

Your Why

'My favourite kind of people are those whose eyes whisper that they've been taken to the edge of their will, the precipice of their sanity, digging into their core to remain standing. For me, they're beauty personified and the most alive of all.'

JESSICA HUIE

When your vision for your life is powered by meaning, you develop superhero strength to step out, be seen and save your own day.

It was a summer's afternoon one Sunday some 13 years ago, when my daughter was six years old. Like me, as a child she'd developed a love for song and dance. On this particular Sunday, she was due to perform a few miles across the city. It was to be an open-air performance exhibiting her progress at dance school that term. I was sick. Laid up with a wretched virus that had me bed-bound. The night before I'd asked her dad to take her to the performance and be present so that one of us could be there to clap. But 1 o'clock came and went, and we became anxious.

She was due to grace the stage at 2 p.m. and the journey would take at least 45 minutes without traffic. By 1:30 p.m., a last-minute text message confirmed he wasn't going to show, so I dragged myself off the sofa, threw on some clothes and called a taxi, planning to use my last £15. I felt so unwell that driving seemed an impossibility and besides, my fuel tank was empty. Parking in that part of London was also a non-starter and given that we were already late, a taxi that we could leap out of on arrival seemed the most sensible option.

The taxi arrived and as we got closer to the venue, it occurred to me that I had no idea how we were going to get back home. My daughter's father's no-show had crushed her, again. I'd gone into protective-mum mode. Performing in the show would be a welcome distraction and sick or not, I needed to be watching from the crowd. She danced and smiled in return, but as the show ended, the reality that we now had a five-mile journey back home and no money came back to me.

This was a period of my life when I was a like a crab in a bucket, working all hours to crawl out of the circumstances we were in whilst trying to navigate life as a single parent, struggling to manage my daughter's emotions as her father consistently failed to show up. It hurt. Each time she was hurt by another arrangement missed, I lived her pain. Like an infected wound that doesn't heal, I internalized her disappointment, viewing it as a failure on my part to protect my daughter from the reality of our family life.

It was the small things like the parents' evenings and the first day of school that compounded this feeling of failure.

Often, my dad would accompany me, as I learned early of the awkwardness of being the youngest mother in the room by 10 years and without a husband to converse with. I stuck out like a sore thumb and yearned to have the domestic perfection these families seemed to have. I didn't fit. I felt constantly judged. And the biggest condemnation came from myself.

So on this sunny afternoon, while the skies were blue and the crowd of adoring parents beamed with pride, I was beginning to panic. I couldn't bear for my daughter to know the sad truth that Mummy had no money to get us home, for that would've been the hardest pill to swallow. To be seen by my child, someone so dependent and adoring, as somehow inept and incapable. Looking back, I wonder why I hadn't called on my parents for help. But at that time I was so consumed by having something to prove to them and the rest of the world, those who I felt had written me off, and not wanting to be a burden, that I'd make difficult situations even more difficult. Perhaps if the venue had been closer and I hadn't felt so unwell that I feared my legs would cave, we would've walked – the miles passed off as a bear hunt or search for the yellow brick road.

Emotionally, the hours of waiting for him to show up had weakened my spirit. I was trying, really trying, so hard to keep the cogs turning towards a better day. I was fragile and exhausted, yet the journey was just beginning. So with a prayer and my cheque book and debit card in my bag, we flagged a taxi and I sat awkwardly for 25 minutes, sipping water to prevent the nausea and part virus, part life, rising up in my chest.

'Do you accept cheques for payment?' I asked timidly, already knowing the answer.

I was good for it. I would be paid from my magazine job in just a few days and if this taxi driver would only allow me to exchange a cheque in payment for the fare home, his funds would duly hit his account in the days to come.

'No. Cash only.'

Alas, my card would be declined anyway, for there were no spare pound coins in my account for rainy days. No holiday money saved for tomorrow. Every pound was accounted for, as being mum and dad to my daughter while attempting to be financially independent from the state allowed nothing for savings accounts.

The words exchanged during that final five minutes of the taxi ride are no longer available to me. I only recall blurred moments of him pulling up outside a police station and shouting, enraged, before deeming the walk into the station to report my £30 offence unworthy of his time. He simply told us to get out. And we did. Me suppressing tears, with this precious bewildered girl whose eyes I couldn't meet.

We walked the remaining 20 minutes of the journey home, silently comforting one another. I wished he'd accepted the cheque. I didn't want his time to have been wasted, his service to have been abused. It was an afternoon which, amidst a period of constantly reaching for better, for more, both practically and developmentally, sent me crashing into

152

shame. I felt like nothing. Just nothing. And it was from this place of shameful nothingness – after tears and prayers and the embrace of a mother determined that her daughter would never again be reduced to an involuntary walk home – a fire called grit began to build. Along with a hardness that would carry me suffocatingly through countless other tests of will.

Hardness is different to strength and after a significant period of time, I've softened. The years have taught me that true strength lies in vulnerability and I no longer need to battle my way through life. Monet Huie – with her brown eyes, curly hair and a smile that lit up the world – was my *why*. This child, whose entrance to the world became the reason for my continued existence and the motivation for my achievement, gave me fuel. My desire for her to have a life of opportunity became the cause for which I was fighting.

On many occasions I would crumple into a ball of questioning, wanting to quit. The strain of the parental role, combined with the tests of my burgeoning career on a girl in a woman's body, was a feeling that was too much to bear. Monet was the why that made me write for an extra hour, leave the office later in order to rise through the ranks and earn more money, complete the degree, secure the client, disrupt the high street. My *why* was non-negotiable, unquestionable. And so armed with a reason to excel that was wrapped around my heart came the will to succeed.

Now that *why* has grown into a beautiful young woman – who, coincidentally, remembers the taxi incident well – and become a desire to improve the prospects of others, particularly the marginalized, and it's a purpose that lights up my soul. The importance of my *why* is critical, because without this reason, I could opt for the smoother road and the quick buck, but at a compromise to my truth. Having a *why* that turns on the part of you that connects you with the world is critical, as seeing any goal through to fruition requires steel, so you'll need a significant reason to keep going when it gets tough.

Like the child who saw himself reflected in my Color blind greetings cards and the people whose thank-you cards today decorate my mantel, it's the impact of one human being on another that overrides any financial prize. Combining your purpose with contribution is the sweet spot where you'll dive out of bed to begin your day, your work will become your joy and you'll experience true fulfilment.

Atticus, named after Atticus Finch in *To Kill a Mockingbird*, is a brand-new soul food dining room launched by Iqbal Wahhab CBE, the entrepreneur behind two of London's most successful restaurants, Roast and The Cinnamon Club – add both to your 'must visit' list if you haven't already been culinarily acquainted. Atticus, however, is no ordinary restaurant and Iqbal no typical entrepreneur. Atticus, which at the time of writing is no more than a business plan and a concept, is on a mission to create a movement. A movement illustrating that by giving business a powerful *why* as its engine, we *all* win. For Atticus, the movement is based around the entrenched belief that business can increasingly prove it's a force for good. A Bangladeshi man, Iqbal started life as a gang member in South London. Of the former group of five best friends from school, three ended up in jail and one committed suicide. For

Iqbal, employing ex-offenders isn't an opportunity to gain brownie points for corporate social responsibility; it's a soul-driven obligation and a nod to his own blessings.

Before coming up with the plan for Atticus – a restaurant aiming to create a social momentum that drives other businesses to infuse purpose at their core – Iqbal spent time away from running his companies to see how the business community could have a significant impact in reducing reoffending rates when it came to crime. This in turn led to him offering work placements to prisoners on day release, which became so successful that many went on to work for him on completion of their sentences.

Everything from how the restaurant selects its people – a large proportion of whom will be employed through partnerships with organizations who train ex-offenders and refugees to be employment-ready – to its produce will stem from these values. Values born out of a desire to empower, support and improve both individual lives and society as a whole. Values that are indivisible from the beliefs of the man driving this fried chicken and waffle heaven – a perfect example of where the professional output of a person becomes perfectly in tune with the belief systems at their core. This is purpose in HD.

'Atticus is not a charity or a social enterprise; the future of our planet lies in the hands of business. It's down to us to fix the many problems we often created. The good news for cynics of such an approach is that time and again those of us who have adopted this method have seen a greater return on the wallet

than those who don't. That's the ultimate (though previously unverified when we first embarked on this journey) beauty of purpose – it doesn't distract from the pursuit of profit, but actually enhances it.'
IQBAL WAHHAB CBE

I think the future will see social enterprise become a non-entity as businesses infused with social contribution become the norm rather than the niche. If you're starting from a blank canvas then you have the opportunity to use your business or career as a vessel for contribution, delivering a profit that not only feeds into a life of your ideal design, but also feeds your soul. What's exciting is that your customers will respond to your cause, because the values that encapsulate it will resonate and speak to *their* values, resulting in an authentic momentum that no contrived marketing campaign could contend with.

Let go of the pursuit of riches and immerse yourself in service of the bigger goal. It's not about neglecting bills, which of course still need to be paid, but about doing what you have to do until you can afford to do what you want to do. Living a life of meaning isn't just reserved for the privileged, who have the luxury of time and money to ponder their purpose, and I'm the first to understand what it means to struggle, but that is all the more reason to transcend the hamster wheel of survival. When your goal goes beyond the benefit of you alone, financial success and recognition will often be the deserved by-product, but you have to have faith in and commit to your vision in order not to compromise on your legacy. Trust that when you're on the path that's meant for you, you'll be supported by the universe.

Let your *why* form the foundation of your enterprise, and your cause and its meaning will keep your ship afloat through rough seas. This will enable you to smile at your reflection each morning, content in the knowledge that your worthiness stems not from the car you drive nor your bank balance, but from who you are. Our challenges are ripe for leveraging, for our breakdowns can be our greatest breakthroughs. In falling apart, there's the opportunity for our rebuilding with stronger material, soul power and a new reliance on our inner guidance to map out our route.

Find
Your Voice

'Find your voice and inspire others to find theirs.'
STEPHEN COVEY

Armed with your *why*, step into the spotlight and own who you are. The new day is almost here. Can you feel it? The rumble of change manifesting itself in political upheaval, social discord and uprising, globally. The present moment feels to me like a worldwide vomit. As though the planet can no longer digest the processed diet it's been existing on. We've overdosed on technology, designed to bring us closer together, and yet we're more isolated than ever before. The desire for money and power has superseded the care of humanity, and many of the world's heinous crimes stem from this misplaced belief of who and what is valued.

We are a world with a spiritual deficit created by millions of people who are clueless as to who they really are. People swarming fearfully around trying to protect their status, territory and belongings, sleeping with one eye open. The world needs a new mindset for the new era, and all the findings back up the fact that purpose and meaning are the new black. In the past couple of years, there's been a widespread rejection of having to conform to outdated ways of working, farcical 'have it all' notions that misrepresent what 'it all' is, and we're finally reconsidering what we want to do.

Month after month, my workshops at the British Library are full of people who've rejected this corporate glass-breaking idea of old, because actually as they climbed the stairs they found the view less than appealing. Whilst the last political year has unquestionably turned up the fear gauge to alarming proportions, the housing crisis – meaning many will never own their home – the increasing divide between rich and poor, strained public health services and increasing mental illness means uncertainty prevails. At least when we were in a recession there was the prospect of emergence, but in this new age of unpredictability, none of us have any idea what awaits humanity around the corner. So we have choices. To immerse ourselves in the madness, digest the increasingly alarming news, or baton down our personal hatches and seek out the truth that lies within ourselves whilst contributing our light to the world...

Those same growing pains that we experience as we shed our skin and step into the greater 'woken' version of ourselves are being experienced collectively. People are no longer willing to squeeze themselves into boxes. We demand to bring all of who we are to work and to be valued, having our individuality honoured, accepted and included. So while big business scrambles to change its culture or risk losing its future employees and customers, data and statistics are surfacing each day confirming what we can already intrinsically feel – we're on the cusp of a new dawn.

All of a sudden, the power is with the people. Corporations are caught playing catch-up with the reality that as a result of an ageing workforce and restrictive migration policy, they may soon not have enough people to fill the roles that require them.

All of the political leaders who've seen success over the past two years have boldly stated a position. Often, these positions have divided the world and will continue to do so, but note how the unapologetic verbalization has replaced the old sanitized and far safer political speech of old. Whoever you are – politician, freelancer, small or multinational business owner – the message ringing out from all thought leadership and research is common. Values and purpose must underpin your vehicle and therefore your message.

Having spent a lifetime in communications, I've turned 360 degrees from the world of sanitized and contrived showbiz PR to a commitment to speak the truth. Helping organizations and entrepreneurs to define their message and speak their purpose is a topic I'm passionate about. It's been thrilling to find that the concept of purpose with profit is one that many business leaders are already embedding into their business DNA. Individuals who get that diversity isn't a fragmented group of individuals over *there*, but in fact *all of us*. Bold leaders who understand that at the root of creating a culture that includes and honours its respective members, is a need to let go of the separation that has divided us as human beings and communities for too long. A need to listen with the intent to understand, rather than the intent to reply. Business leaders with the courage to do things differently and to believe the unthinkable will help the world to redefine what success looks like. History concurs. The Luther King Jrs, the Einsteins, the Gandhis, the Malala Yousafzais, the Marie Curies: examples of what can be achieved when we question the status quo, welcome resistance, become accountable, embrace visibility and boldly speak our truth.

The size and perceived importance of the entity in which we find our voice is as irrelevant as our role. All that matters is what's powering us. And as we move from ambition to meaning, we'll see the impact begin to flow out from within the organizations where it was birthed, into broader society. The new success is about creating a life of fulfilment. Standing for something. Representation, awareness, accountability, connection, equality, truth.

Hay House Publishers are in the business of publishing books, but their mission is to change lives. Apple is a tech company, but Steve Jobs' original mission statement declared that the company's purpose was to contribute to the world by making tools that advance humankind. The Body Shop, started in 1976 by the late Anita Roddick, sells body products – but its mission is to enrich lives and the planet.

Often, the individuals who come to my 'Raise your Profile' workshops are running small or microbusinesses selling products or services that on the surface have nothing particularly original or innovative about them. My role is to scratch beneath the surface and keep scratching until I arrive at the epicentre of these enterprises. What are these individuals, who've courageously taken earning a living into their own hands, really up to?

I've been excited to find that in 100 per cent of the cases where I get to speak to the business owner, there's always a meaningful *why* buried beneath the wrapping of the business bumf about the product. The problem is that in a marketplace flooded with choice, nobody cares about greetings cards, and there are a million different bath salts and body butters I can slather on. It's always the *why* people buy, as their purchase is an opportunity to invest in their own belief systems and create instant all-round feel-good.

Most of us know this conceptually, but as we start our businesses, it's easy to get caught up in the day-to-day running of it – and all the materials, logos and packages – and we lose sight of the heartbeat, the soul of the business, which is the very story we need to be telling. In other cases, I've found that it's only in the real time of the workshop, as I lead people back in history over the steps that led to them starting their business, that they've even become aware of the very reason they're doing what they're doing. An 'aha' moment occurs because they've stepped outside of their enterprise and are looking in at it through a new lens.

Communicating your mission or *why* across all of your marketing is a key part of embracing visibility. Nobody cares about what you do – for we're all too busy with what *we* do – but we do care about *why* you do it. People will care about your journey and the steps that brought you to today. They will connect with you, the human behind the website, on a level that no product or packaging can compete with. We're all intrinsically connected, individual droplets in one big universal ocean. So when your truth speaks to mine, I hear it.

The first time I spoke up in a way that really pushed me beyond the safety of my boundaries, it felt like a complete watershed moment:

'We have a culture of mistrust in this agency.'

Silence.

My voice shook as I continued, 'The impact on the team is that nobody feels safe and so they apportion blame on one another and gossip because they're afraid for the security of their role. And it's unhealthy for us both as individuals and as a company. It's toxic, for all of us. We need to address it.'

Still silence.

The conversation hadn't been a part of the boss's plan. We were there to talk strategy, targets, roles and responsibilities, and I was flagging an office culture of moral deficit. My speech wasn't received particularly well. Defences went up and as the silence prevailed, I was alone in my stand for integrity. But damn it! I've never felt more liberated, more real.

Speaking your truth will set you free like that. How could we address figures and success formulas if we sidelined the decay in the very foundation that was eroding the good work, morale and productivity of our collective efforts? By the time I made it home that evening, I was breathless. I sat, coat still on, in the bathroom and sobbed between gasps for breath, the sobs rising from a place deep within me. Tears for every difficult conversation I'd ever, or never, had. For all of the times I'd suppressed the thing I *needed* to say but didn't for fear of ejection from a group or by a person or because of being stigmatized.

The tears weren't of pain but of euphoria. They stemmed from the most powerful feeling of relief. As though I'd climbed a steep hill and finally reached the top, where the air was clear and oxygen now filled my thirsty lungs. I smiled, between sobs, at the boldness of who I was becoming.

That moment when I spoke up, I'd taken another step up the staircase towards becoming *more* of me. A staircase on which awkward silences, resistance and not belonging came with the territory. To me, the journey towards belonging meant accepting that the trade-off would often mean not fitting in with others. Just to utter the words in an environment where my language might well have been alien, had taken me digging deep into my core. But once I'd spoken these words, I could not and would not be muted.

When you find your voice, you're no longer concerned about alienating yourself from others. The need to fit in or to be in keeping with the clan is pushed to one side to make way for *your* truth – and this is liberation. And while your voice may shake as you step hesitantly into this new terrain, on arriving you'll find the land is steady, the ground beneath your feet certain. The earth will wrap around your roots with a certainty that confirms every fibre of your self. You'll know who you are and you'll be unwavering, unapologetic. Fear will drip away. So one day you'll wake up and find all you have is who your soul cries out for you to be, and then nothing can be taken from you. No career, no relationship, no life that doesn't allow for your truest expression of being to take shape is a compromise worthy of such a grave sacrifice. Build from that point and your house is solid. When you live in truth you need nothing, you're already complete.

This confidence speaks before you do and in a world in which compromise is the norm, it stands out as not of this world, sparking one of two reactions: magnetism or resistance. Our job is to brush the latter off our shoulders and refuse to cave in to the compelling human need to fit. You were born to stand out. Be an outlier. And as with authenticity, you'll spark a light in your sister or brother to awaken them to their own truth. And one by one, we can trigger the shift into a collective world evolution.

Surrender

*'Transformation happens on the
other side of surrender.'*
UNKNOWN

To truly find your voice is to be awake, to be in the moment, present to the boundless truth of who we are and detached from the limitations of an existence hemmed by identification with ourselves as merely physical bodies. Our awareness at this level allows for a broadening of our perceptions, and we become receptive to insights and discoveries that have always been there, but were beyond our periphery within our unenlightened existence.

Challenge is a blessing. When we're discontent, pained, excluded or sick we're more likely to turn our faces to the sun, to explore alternatives and exits from our reality. Those who bob along through their lives in a constant comfortable meander have less incentive to dig beneath the surface to shake up their norm. While life may be devoid of euphoric highs, they're spared the lows that test the spirit, and encourage, coerce and call it into surrender. In this way, challenge becomes our greatest blessing and our doorway to serenity. However, I didn't know that when 'Daddy', as my brothers and I called him right up until his departure, was diagnosed with terminal cancer.

Life without Dad was incomprehensible to me really, as silly as that may sound. He was an older parent, me the eldest of three and alike him in so many ways, from the fiery temper that had quelled with the years to a no-nonsense intolerance for the idle or the irreverent. I adored him, as many daughters do, but more. I got him and he got me, and we enjoyed a soul connection, which meant that I didn't have to say anything for him to know when all wasn't well.

In a childhood much like your favourite three-legged chair – precious yet so unstable it threatened to bruise you each time it collapsed – Dad was the invisible fourth leg. The strength. My stability, my world. And into adulthood it was as though mere moments in his presence could calm an apocalypse. My safe place.

I wasn't ready for him to die even at 82. Nor was he. And he said as much, which made it harder. The idea of existence without my dad didn't just terrify me, it seemed impossible, for our relationship was intrinsic to my identity.

Somehow, I'd expected death in old age to mean a person would accept open-armed that their time had come, gracefully and bravely. I discovered that it doesn't always happen that way... Life, as Dad said, was 'the best it had ever been', and that perhaps is what hurt most.

'I'm not going to be here forever you know,' my dad would say before he became ill. Looking over from his living-room throne he'd grin, laughing with his hearty but gentle chuckle. Looking at me in amusement, but also for reassurance that I was aware of the fact and, even more so, would be able to cope with it. I'd roll my eyes affectionately and change the subject, refusing to engage in what I saw then as his morbid dialogue, and we'd get back to our evening.

My dad's illness progressed quickly, and he died within six months of being diagnosed with cancer. The diagnosis came out of the blue as three generations of our family were preparing to return to the island of his birth for my nuptials, and watching him come to terms with his approaching death felt like being in a bubble that floated in a different dimension to the rest of the world. I felt the weight of his angst as tangibly as if it were my own body being ravaged by cancer. As though it was me attempting to comprehend detachment from a life of ten thousand stories, and a family for whom I was the epicentre.

I was completely submerged in the experience with Dad, as though our separation had ceased and I had somehow become one with him. Our interaction in those last weeks was unlike anything I have known – pure.

It was a conversation between souls, not people. An exchange of love between two spirits, not a father and daughter. In day-to-day life, our communications are dictated and constrained by time, roles, expectations and motives. There was none of that. This was less of a conversation and more of a spiritual dance. A dance that at times was painfully raw yet beautiful in the honesty of its love.

The tension knitted into my shoulders and back, and my skin broke out in lumps. Yet within the suffering there was bliss.

As Dad's appetite lapsed, my brothers, Mum and I would ply him with smoothies and liquid meals. But the more ill he became, the less he could stomach. One day I received a message from my brother who was preparing to leave the hospital where he had been with our father, saying that dad had requested ice cream. I had been to the hospital that morning and was physically spent, but this was a big deal – our dad's first request to eat in many weeks. I jumped in the car, ice cream in tow.

I will never forget seeing my father's face and aura light up at the sight of me, ice cream in hand. He didn't expect to see me again that day, less still with the ice cream. Everything was wrong about this picture: the fragility of the body of this man who could stand on his head until the age of 70, and the sterile space in which he now seemed so small. Yet he beamed, and I felt his love pour out from his soul and fill me up from the inside, so that I stood there encased and overflowing with the light of our love. Words cannot do justice to the feeling of true unconditional, selfless love. It takes your breath away. This is where *true* joy lives, I thought.

After an hour or two I floated out of the hospital, and to my delight found the Macmillan band playing on the ground floor, trumpets lighting up the air with the most passionate music of love and hope, soothing the many hearts breaking within the hospital walls. More tears rolled.

A life spent trying to pre-empt things that might go wrong, and working to make things happen, was pointless in the face of cancer. With all my power and might, when I ran out of resistance, there was nothing I could do but accept the situation. For the first time in my life, I was forced to shuffle over into the passenger seat, buckle my seatbelt and breathe. I wasn't the driver for this journey and the route was unknown.

One day I visited the wonderful Macmillan centre, where I got to know a kind lady working there who happened to be married to a Jamaican man. She'd given me a recipe for Guinness punch, one of my dad's favourite island drinks, only this one was made up with the Ensure weight-gain drink the hospital prescribed. On this particular day I'd decided I needed to know how much longer we had with our dad. The doctors hadn't told us, of course nobody knows conclusively, but it was April, my wedding in Jamaica was due to happen the following month and more than anything I wanted my father to walk me down the aisle. Not for me, for him. I knew what it meant to a man whose life was built on family. He'd given everything to raise us with my mother, so he deserved that joy.

Already fighting tears even before the words had been uttered, given my dad's prognosis, and based on her broad experience supporting cancer sufferers and their families, I asked how long Dad might have left to live. Her response stunned me... three months.

I unravelled.

My husband and I began to consider plan B – a registry office wedding in London in case Dad couldn't travel. It's funny that wedding planning is a control freak's field day, with all the flowers and favours and entertainment and planners to arrange. I had lighting and videography, guest welcome bags for the near 100 guests travelling from across the world and a honeymoon in Bali booked to follow the big day. It was to be at one of the most exquisite venues on the island, but when the prospect that Dad might not be there was raised, it all meant nothing. I'd have got married by his hospital bedside if necessary. And my husband, God bless him, understood and was in agreement.

And so in one of the most meaningful interactions of my existence, this woman I'd spoken to no more than three times said, 'I know it's hard to believe now, but some of the moments at the end can be very special – the most special of all.' I was too numb to digest the statement fully, but I'd heard her.

This stranger gave me permission to begin to let go, to surrender to what life was serving. From that moment, acceptance slowly began to embrace me. And with it came an end to the resistance and fighting against what the universe was presenting. I couldn't control whether or not my dream wedding on the island would go ahead and nor could I control whether or not my dad would attend. There was nothing to do but make the journey as comfortable as possible, so with much praying and many tears, I stepped into the fog and began to let go.

Dad did make it to Jamaica for my wedding. We walked down the aisle together and he embraced my husband at the altar in a manner that felt like a poignant handover. We danced together to Louis Armstrong's 'What a Wonderful World', oblivious to our guests and the cameras that captured three miraculous minutes as we cried silently together. Though the gravity of my father's condition tested us all, it was sheer magic to see him surrounded by his grandchildren on the island of his birth, gathered together for my wedding day.

After our return to England the disease became more aggressive and, for me, the world beyond Dad's needs ceased to exist. I detached myself from the illusion of a life and demands that just months before had seemed so pressing.

I knew the prognosis before I arrived. I'd called in that morning to plead with the nurses to delay the consultant's visit with my dad until I could be present to cushion the bleak finality, if such a thing is possible. None of my darkest moments have come close to that day, when I drove to the hospital to be at my father's side while the consultant informed him that the cancer was rampaging through his body and the end was near.

In the weeks leading up to that day I'd come to see the child in my father. This small, vulnerable boy preparing to venture to an unknown plane. No longer a daughter, roles blurred, boundaries dissolved, I'd become more than Dad's carer – I'd become his backbone. My life had become a schedule of scans and consultant appointments, and with my family's support I was unfailingly at his side. And yet this final destination was not one to which I could accompany him. Helplessness enveloped me.

In a hospital car park, entirely out of character, I looked to the sky and asked my ancestors to give me strength so that my legs wouldn't cave and my demeanour crumble, so I might be who I needed to be for my father that morning. I know that my request, born from a space of utter surrender and complete honest need, was heard that morning. A presence walked with me to the ward where my father awaited.

I thought I knew love, but barring the purity of childbirth, my love, like most, had been self-seeking, driven by a need for reciprocity, for comfort, for reassurance. The love I discovered in those precious weeks caring for Dad was selfless and unadulterated. Its force filled the room and though silent, it resounded for all to hear – an outpouring from my soul. And though it hurt – it hurt so much the ache in my chest was physical – it was a beautiful pain. Love was the truth, the only truth. And its tangible presence took my breath away.

I discovered that our greatest learning and growth comes not from the situations in which we are steering the ship, but when we surrender to the force so much bigger than ourselves. Also when we trust that the universe will lead us to a destination where love, peace and miracles beyond comprehension show up in our lives.

Our challenge? To be willing to believe and step courageously onto the path, without knowing where it might lead. To trust that there's so much more than that which we can see or touch. To have faith that when your life seems as though it's falling apart, the likelihood is that the universe is deliberately cracking you open, so that you can emerge butterfly-like into awakening.

Become Who You Are

'Become who you are.'
RASHEED OGUNLARU

I finally began to become who I am in the unearthly, profound days between life and death.

The attribute that is grace is not something I'd ever given thought to, but aged 36, ejected from the endemic buzz of my non-stop life, we came face to face. I'm doubtful that the four carers who alternated the days they attended my dad at the home I grew up in have any idea quite what they did for me and my family. In the corner sits a 2-metre- (7-foot-) high plant as old as I am, one of many much-loved plants that my green-fingered mum tends to. There are framed pictures everywhere, 50 or more in unmatched frames, all capturing our family moments. My parents' living room is sort of the tropics meet Morocco. An antithesis to the symmetrical show home. Chaotically pristine and as cosy as they come. Pics of my brother aged five chasing a chicken in Jamaica, me aged 11, all frizzy hair and skinny legs. The adored grandchildren, all smiles and love over nearly 40 years, everywhere.

In the corner of the room is a worn leather office chair. A chair from which the occupier could lord over the room quite comfortably, commanding attention and ears in need of reprimanding or recharging. The fabric is torn in a few places, but the chair still so fit for use and comfortable that its proud owner wasn't ready to forgo it. From this throne, Christmas presents through three decades were unwrapped and later grandbabies spun around to joyous squeals. Phone calls bearing the baddest, saddest and gladdest of news were received on this chair. But now it's vacant.

Before he left us, having come home for his final days, my father lay in a hospital bed in the centre of the room, still centre stage, surrounded by family. And while the room was recognizable, the family within were far from it.

'I don't know, but everything just looks so beautiful...' he said as he gazed, with his eyes glazed over, at the flowers through the balcony door in front of which his hospital bed was positioned. There was a distance in his voice, and a sense of awe and surprise in his tone. I watched him picking at his sheets and recognized the action from the 'signs your relative is near death' end-of-life booklet I'd already memorized. 'I can't seem to stop picking at these sheets,' he said. 'It's the drugs,' Mum told him. 'No, I think I'm going somewhere...' he said.

He was, and a week later he did. What I didn't expect was that a great chunk of the person I used to identify as, would go with him.

⌒

Over the course of that period – amidst a noisy buzz of doctors, nurses and individuals delivering hospital equipment – four individuals entered my parents' home to accompany us as we maintained a bedside vigil beside my daddy. Rahul and his colleagues entered spaces where they witnessed the rawness of emotion at its purest, as a small family attempted to cope with the idea of a 30-year-old chair that would never again seat its family commander.

Supporting us was part of their job, and yet the gentleness, care and dignity with which they performed their respective roles, even in the midst of hearts cracking into pieces, blew my mind. In the last days when words began to fail me, when I dared not speak lest the floodgates open and the torrent building in my heart sink me, these four individuals whispered the words that I could say, giving gentle nudges of stories I could remind him of. And I did.

These individuals' job description came without a script and yet in this naked setting, where the only goal is to enable another human being to leave the world as comfortably as possible, their way of being was the most beautiful thing I ever witnessed. They entered and departed our home with a reverence becoming of the circumstances. While it may sound trite, so many of the others who attended during those weeks would be confronted by the protective lion cub I became for my father. 'Please lower your voice.' 'Remove your shoes.' 'This isn't a patient; he's my father and the greatest man I've ever known.' But these four introduced me to true selfless beauty and the human capacity for who we can be for one another, in even the most testing circumstance. And the grace in these four angels awakened me to the grace within myself.

In the final days I began to write. And at 3 a.m. one morning in the spare room of my parents' house, where my dad lay downstairs on a hospital bed, one of the hospice carers seated at his side, the following stream of consciousness landed on the page:

All lights are out bar the light of a candle's glow. The living room is now empty, family having dispersed, and only Rahul – the softly spoken Bangladeshi carer from the hospice – and I remain. He will accompany me through the night at dad's bedside, allowing me the respite of an hour or two to sleep.

I sit as close to the bed as possible, the thought of climbing up, lying beside him and nestling my head in his armpit returning to my mind over and over. I discard it. The time for that has passed – he is too frail now and the slightest touch is painful. So instead I place my cheek as close as possible to his hand, so that my eyelashes brush his knuckle, then I close my eyes and envelop myself in the sound of his breath. Drinking it in, I consider recording this precious sound for future use. Future power, future fuel for my soul. I discard the idea and smile at the absurdity of the thought. Cuddles and congruent conversation now a thing of the past – last week! And each breath takes us closer to his last. Yet, in this present moment is beauty.

I close my eyes and am transported 27 or so years back to a night I lay pretending to sleep in my bed. Hearing his voice answer and end a phone call, I knew full well he was coming to my room to wake me. It felt like midnight, but it was probably closer to 9 p.m. – long past my bedtime at seven or eight years old. Earlier that day, in a moment of jealousy, I'd taken my best friend's fuchsia pink satin, fur-lined jacket from her school peg and dunked it in one of the girls' toilets, leaving it there until she tracked it down at 3:30 p.m., teary and perplexed. Our family didn't have money for such luxuries, and I'd been overcome by envy and self-pity.

Dad woke me gently, asked me whether I was responsible, stressed the importance of honesty and the ugliness of a lie, and urged me to respond with truth. Confession served, he then told me to get dressed and marched me, quietly but unswervingly, to Danielle's house. The night walk of shame was long, and I can still recall the heaviness of heart and the uncomfortableness of having been caught out, now faced with confronting my actions. On arrival, I was to confess and apologize to Danielle wholeheartedly. And never, ever was I to express envy towards another again.

So I did – and magic happened. During the walk home I was a lighter little Jessica. I had no idea then that this lesson in self-responsibility, this commitment to truth, this utter non-negotiable requirement for integrity, had been taught to me that night and the seed of a value planted firm.

These beautiful moments of reflection, epiphanies and buried memories that floated to the surface of my consciousness in the weeks since my father's condition deteriorated, have come as all boundaries and awkwardness are stripped away.

Finding a layer of strength I didn't know existed, in order to contend with his brutal pain and to care for his most basic human needs, has unearthed a love more profound than anything I could've imagined. I've given birth twice and I thought life experience had taught me all its secrets, but joy, there is more.

'The fog is rising, let us venture in,' as the saying goes. But it has risen, and as I immerse myself in the raw grief of losing the individual who is my lighthouse, the reward is transformational. Dad continues to teach me my most valuable lessons.

Every tear, every moment of despair, is worth the joy and learning I've found in caring for and loving my dying father. I'm forever changed. I've found there's sheer joy wrapped within pain, strength in exposing oneself to raw grief and a love, a joyous love too engulfing to be of this world, waiting for those willing to explore despair.

The fog will rise – venture in.

Each day, step out with intention to bring your thoughts and actions in line with that ultimate version of the person you intend to become. Let the qualities you admire in others be a reminder of that same light within you.

And when you revert to your old self, because you will, be gentle with yourself, with the same tenderness you'd afford a child. Nurture yourself mentally, physically and spiritually with the soul food you need to blossom into the person you always were before life chiselled you into hardness or submission. And as you bloom, watch in wonder as the world responds to your new song, meeting you at your new level, your new line, your raised bar.

With every step, let your majesty be felt, own your presence. Step forth with your power and an aura that announces that you fully claim the greatness from which you were birthed and need no permission. Let your quiet power announce that you've arrived before you even enter the room. Own it, with strength, with grace, with humility. This road isn't easily travelled and my friend, you deserve it all.

There's More

'Those who have failed to work toward the truth have missed the purpose of living.'
BUDDHA

*'Is it his spirit I feel in the wind wistfully
swaying the branches of the trees?*

In the stare of the fox who frequents our garden?

In the scent of the honeysuckle climbing the wall?

*In the soft lilt of the waves encompassing
me in the Caribbean Sea?*

*Is the breeze that brushes my face on my
morning walk the hand that stroked my
hair as a child to lull me into sleep?*

*Though the absence of his human presence has
left a crater in my world, his spirit surrounds me
in all that I do and so we're closer than ever.*

*The divisions of humankind removed, replaced
with a closeness without separation.*

*Just as he's stepped on to connect with the
infinite wonder of the universe, so have I.*

*That untapped part of me so long dormant,
now awakened, so that my heart meets every
blade of grass and merges with its energy.*

*And within that connection to all that
is, I'm not the same woman.*

I am everywoman and everything.

Just as you are every person and everything.

*I have, for fleeting moments, glimpsed
nirvana and its sweet nectar.'*

JESSICA HUIE

The day before my father's last on this Earth, I moved with a quiet power. My parents still lived on the West London estate where we'd grown up on the fifth and highest floor. On that morning before Dad's last, I became conscious of the various noises signifying that life outside of our surreal four walls of unwatched clocks marched onwards. Next door, new carpets being laid. Downstairs on the ground floor, garden furniture being built, beckoning the imminent summer weeks. I excused myself and as though God Herself was carrying me, I knocked on each door requesting that carpet laying and garden furniture building be put on hold, so that my father might have the reverence of quiet. People are mostly very kind, I have found, and one by one the bustle of continued life outside of our window ceased.

When I was four years old, my dad wrote me a note saying that he hoped I'd 'grow to be a person of humility and selflessness, for in that I would know the joy of living'. A miracle then, that rooted in the passenger seat of his bodily journey out of this world, I came to experience the meaning of his wish.

That morning, short of air, I left my parents' house and walked to Whiteleys, the local shopping centre. I needed clothes. I'd been staying at my parents' home for the past few days and needed a change of outfit. I didn't really, but it gave me a cause for the walk. Travelling down the local roads on which I'd walked my whole life, this was a journey like no other. I'd danced down these roads as a teenager at the Notting Hill carnivals, breaking free from childhood and curfews, high on the sheer volume and energy of the crowd. I'd skipped down these very streets to my nursery school with Mum, with the promise of lemon curd sandwiches and Kermit the Frog playtimes awaiting me. I'd even bustled along as a young mum on a mission, on the school run via bus, before the race to the office and the rest of my life. Then there were the date nights in my late twenties, high-heeled and heady with love and lust, with the promise of an evening like no other. These streets had illustrated the stories of my life.

It was a surreal, out-of-body experience this time, as though I didn't occupy the physical form placing one foot in front of the other as I headed towards the bustling Westbourne Grove and on to Bayswater. My phone was in my hand, just in case. And yet I had an innate sense that my father would remain in his medically induced coma, heart continuing to beat, while I took this walk, took in this air. Of course he would.

On entering the shopping centre, I was drawn to a 1.5-metre- (5-foot-) high plant in the florist from which I'd often bought flowers. Strong, tall and tropical, it reminded me of the one that had moved house with my family and which my mother said was older than me. I made a mental note to return for it. Later. The streets were bustling as ever, but for me there was no sound. Even my thoughts were stilled, my heartbeat the only soundtrack.

Back at my parents' flat, my father's breathing had changed, becoming louder and rattling. I returned to the seat at his side, announcing my return but knowing no response would come. I slid my hand back into his, where it had been burrowed for much of the past week, with the exception of breaks to allow other family members their time with him.

At about 2 or 3 p.m. that afternoon, the doorbell sounded and my husband arrived. I announced his arrival. My husband stood behind me in the doorway and within minutes, my father took his last breath. My brother and I told him again of our love, as we had over and over, and my mother cried. In a matter of seconds, I experienced a miracle. I experienced my father's spirit separating from and rising from his body, into the air.

The minutes and hours afterwards are a blur but for my husband and brother dealing with the practicalities that follow death. And then I was driving home. I've no idea if anyone else was in the car or if I was alone. I only recall the palpable feeling of my father's energy in my right hand, the right hand that had been buried in his for the past weeks and days. It was the only thought that occupied my mind – Dad's energy was within me. My hand fizzed.

It was the moment that changed everything. I think that once exposed to truth you can never look back. Extracted from the world as I knew it and from within that space of pure love, the truth revealed itself to me. That moment, though fleeting, shifted all that were once beliefs into firm, unequivocal knowing. There is more...

More to us and our existence than that which we can see and touch. So much more to who we are and therefore who we can become. In experiencing that our souls are truly separate from our bodies, all limitations for our lives are blown into non-existence and this eternal questioning of all that we've been conditioned to believe commences.

I'm no longer the woman I was before that day, 28 June 2016. Nor am I all of who I'm becoming yet. A spiritual explorer, navigating life with new feelings and conflicts, I'm relearning me. For every feeling of alignment I encounter, confronting fears and facing uncertainty, often feeling displaced, it's as though I belong nowhere, as my identification with who I used to be falls away. My path, once a given, is no longer clearly set before me. My ideas are bigger and my beliefs question much of what the world has accepted as its precedent, and some days this new view isolates and excludes me. I'm learning to be OK with being in the wilderness.

Faith is my anchor and so I keep walking in the direction of these wondrous new possibilities, accepting that the challenges are simply doorways to the activation of my latent potential. I turn for comfort to the words of the great minds of idealists and thinkers, who were marginalized because they challenged the status quo and made the masses uncomfortable by having the courage not to fit, not to belong. I'm reminded that far from lost, being in the wilderness means I'm more found than I've ever been.

More than half a century ago, Dr Abraham Maslow discovered that people who feel they have a sense of purpose are living the highest qualities that humanity has to offer. Knowing that it's a desire to improve and change lives through my work, whether through mentoring or baring my soul through the pages of this book, or simply leaving the Uber driver lifted with a smile and heartfelt thank-you for his service, the warmth I'm left with lets me know that I'm living on purpose. I aim to make each day about more than just me and my own benefit. I'm no saint, far from it, but at my best, living this way brings me peace, fulfilment and a chain reaction of joy. And though at moments I feel as though I've completely lost my way, when I lay my head on my pillow each night, there's a new wholeness inside of me. An assuredness that reminds me that I know why I'm on this Earth, even if the route and destination aren't of my jurisdiction – and there's no worldly prestige that can possibly contend with that.

My life has shifted from one grounded in so called 'normality' to being something of a wondrous meander through each day. I still take action, ambitious as ever, but I'm now creating my life with my hand divinely held. Where once I would have passed off the signposts of my intuition as coincidence, now I see the miracles for what they are.

In the weeks after my father passed on, I was confronted almost every day by foxes on the road leading up to my home. The sighting wasn't anything peculiar in suburbia where I live, except that the sightings were accompanied by a feeling I couldn't explain – a sense that there was something more about the way in which the animals looked into my eyes, into my soul, and how close (just a metre on one occasion), they came to me. Whatever the continuous fox run-ins were about, I just know that their presence brought me great comfort. Each day when we crossed paths I would smile knowingly and feel the hurt subside a little; I felt a relief.

One day, weeks later, after a particularly restless night of tears of loss, I went downstairs to make a cup of tea. As the kettle boiled I looked up and out into the garden. There, under my favourite tree, two foxes sat as though they'd been there for some considerable time. They stared straight through my floor-to-ceiling windows, right at me. Right at me. Looking into my eyes, unblinking. I walked closer to the glass doors, but they didn't flinch. Tears of joy began to roll down my face and I couldn't explain why, but I knew. It was a knowing that required no proof or explanation. I felt all that I needed to understand. The magnitude of this knowing rendered my mind useless in that moment. The message was received loud and clear: be at peace.

Overcome by emotion and joy, I ran upstairs to tell my husband. He'd become used to my occasional ramblings about light around trees and special foxes, but this time I didn't need his agreement that something incredibly meaningful and unexplainable through physical worldly terms had just occurred.

It was not until several months later that I stumbled across a web page explaining that the symbolism of the fox revolved around the afterlife. Lore has it that a fox sighting was thought by the Chinese to be a signal from the spirits of the deceased. It came as little surprise, and instead just another heart flutter at the incredible miracles that, though my new openness, I now find available to me.

Whenever my vibration is high I am receptive to these happenings. The moment I neglect my connection to self and get embroiled back in the hamster wheel of doing, I am returned back into the old paradigm and cut off from the spiritual power source which has come to guide my life.

Having found within this new realm the serenity and truth I have spent my whole life searching for, my life today has become an incredible adventure in which possibilities are infinite. When we are willing to hack through our layers of cynicism and fear to seek truth, when we become ready to make our lives an honest, courageous uncompromising expression of who we really are, everything that we desire becomes possible for us.

Writing this book is my coming-out party. This is who I am and this much I know is true, for my knowing stems not just from teachings, courses and books, but also from profound experience – my truth. It's insight that I can no longer, will no longer mask or disguise. Inner conflict and spiritual compromise isn't an outfit I'm willing to wear. And when our body turns to dust and our spirit lifts away to continue its journey, love is the only currency of any true worth. As Oprah would say, this much I know is true.

A New Realm of Possibilities

*'Possibilities exist just beyond
your belief system.'*
UNKNOWN

It's December 2015 and there are four people standing in the line ahead of me. Music rings through the air, the carpet is plush, the surroundings the ultimate in opulence. An orchestra plays and the air is thick with pride, theirs and mine.

Prince Charles is a few feet away. I'm in heels, vintage fascinator on my head, favourite gloss on lips, eyes glistening with life. I *am* vibrancy. But wait, I'm on the platform wearing Adidas, baby in belly, train approaching. Grey train, grey sweater, grey world. The future is fog. What if I stepped off the platform and into oblivion... could there be peace then?

They say that in the moments before you die your life flashes before you; well many of my 36 years flashed through my mind at Buckingham Palace. And I wasn't dying; I was about to step forth to collect my honour from the future King of England.

My concern wasn't what life I could create with no home or prospects to offer the child I carried inside me. It was when to bow my head and what to say to the prince. It was real. And all of the emotions hurtled towards me of each of the last 18 years since my daughter's arrival in this world caused my life as an adult to explode with immediacy.

I could have sobbed with gratitude for the strength, perseverance and support I received to bring me to that moment. Instead, I wiped a quiet tear, avoiding mascaraed eyes, head held higher than it had ever been as I stepped forwards to accept my moment. Looking to my right, I could see my daughter, my angel who's trodden the road at my side, often bearing the weight of my heaviness, now 15 and the epitome of grace. And my parents, side by side and a living testament to love and survival – and there was nobody else in the room but God and us.

This has been a year like no other. The process of writing this book has felt so right that at times my resident saboteur has attempted to persuade me it was wrong. I'm soaring. Doing the very things that feel so good that every fibre in me concurs that it's right. And though the miracles of the past 12 months have belonged to me, I'm still in awe at the profoundness of my past year.

Reaching rock-bottom, grief and heartbreak catapulted me into surrender. And broken open, suddenly truth, immense love, and a oneness and connectivity with all the energy of the universe swooshed into the chasm. A veil has lifted and suddenly so much more than ever before makes sense.

My sisters and brothers, you don't need permission. Stop waiting to be chosen – the time has come for us to choose ourselves. This is the age where we start our own damn record label. We leverage the digital space to launch our own magazines, we bring our creativity to the world through the Internet, we're fashion moguls via Etsy. We take our passion and we Google our way into turning it into profit. Stop diluting your power by waiting to be chosen. Deem *yourself* worthy of a pay rise.

Headhunt *you* and decide that you're worthy of a thriving career, doing what you love and contributing to the existence of others. Our reality begins within the confines of our minds, and therefore we must upgrade our inner setting to one of abundance and possibility.

Decide that you can have a business that allows you to work from a place where the view outside your window fills your heart with joy so that joy filters into the output spilling out into the world. Then create a plan to make that vision a reality. Go out and find the ingredients you're missing to make the next step. Let go of attachment to the destination, and instead make living today a homage to your tomorrow in thought, word and action. Bring all of who you are into your workplace, and spread your love and light to all you interact with, elevating the conversation, empowering the agenda. Decide that regardless of your experience of relationships and marriage thus far, you're worthy and deserving of love, incredible love, both in giving and receiving. I'm talking to me and I'm talking to you. Choose yourself.

My father used to say that we should have an invisible line, a line that dictates an expectation as to how we should be treated and also how we should behave – and we should never allow any human to draw us to stoop beneath our line. Building on my dad's wisdom, I implore you to raise your line way up in the clouds. Decide today that you're one of the greatest people who ever lived. Yes, the greatest. You inspire change, progress and possibility in other individuals with your kind words, warm heart, integrity and grace – and then, dear people, grow into that person.

One of my favourite Maya Angelou writings is the story of how when she was a young woman of 22 with her own young child, her mother stopped her one afternoon to say, 'Baby, I've been thinking and now I am sure. You are the greatest woman I've ever met. You are very kind and very intelligent and those elements are not always found together. Mrs Eleanor Roosevelt, Dr Mary McLeod Bethune and my mother – yes, you belong in that category. Here, give me a kiss.' Maya's response was to consider what would happen if her mother were right. Suppose she really was going to become somebody…

Maya's mother saw the divinity in her daughter long before the rest of the world and, most critically, before Maya herself. And that recognition was an early signpost for a young woman of the magnitude of all that she already was. From that point, it was simply about Maya Angelou stepping into herself and becoming her potential. None of us is born more influential, more dignified, more blessed. Not Maya Angelou, not Florence Nightingale, not Mother Theresa, not Oprah Winfrey. In their own individual ways, these women have influenced the world, but we all have the capacity to be beacons of light and inspiration, and to create our own legacy. It's just a question of recognizing that the light we see in others is within ourselves in equal measure, if only we dust off the diamonds that we are and allow ourselves to shine.

Dad would ask me how I was and how things were going each time I saw him. Not in that superficial way, where the asker is simply waiting for confirmation that all is well before moving the conversation back to themselves, but really wanting and waiting to hear of my state of being. He would sit slightly forwards on his chair or with an upright posture and nod his head slowly, his entire body receptive to whatever it was that I had to share.

Dad had this way of making me feel as though there were gold in every one of my syllables. As though I were imparting critical information on which the world depended. His entire attention would focus on me or whoever the subject of his interaction was. He was a glorious listener who, without needing to say it, left you feeling as though all you had to say was valid, important and worthy. It was a little bit of magic. To listen wholly without the need to respond or be heard is a power. As human beings, so often we're generally on the defensive, ready with our response even before having fully digested the verbal offering of those to whom we're speaking. To really listen is to give a gift that says you're worthy of my ear and therefore worthy. Imagine who we could empower both in and outside of our homes if we developed this skill!

Australian Mr Adams was a fabulous listener. He was a temp teacher who showed up for a day when I was seven and our regular teacher was off sick, and he was magical. From the moment he stepped into the class and withdrew a brown paper bag from his satchel, I was captivated. One day he explained that today would be a long story-writing competition – and for the winner, an item from his crisp paper bag awaited. And so we were encouraged into a blissful day, in which our young imaginations took over and we were let off the leash to roam free.

I'm smiling as I write this. I can feel the glee in my little heart as I was given permission to escape to worlds of possibility beyond my reality. Those were tough days. My father was silently coming to terms with the loss of his son, who was abducted aged three whilst with his mother in Australia. He was never found. Just a few years later, my parents met and my mother fell pregnant with me. My mother was also carrying her own pain. We were shielded from my parents' past, except that Mum sought her escape through alcohol and Dad expressed his frustration through anger levelled at Mum. Beautiful, weary souls struggling through their own pain – they did *more* than their best with the cards they'd been dealt.

But age seven was tough. And that day my escape was in the form of Mr Adams. I don't remember the story that I wrote, but remember the pride as I was invited to the front of the class, where this wonderful teacher removed a hologram red-and-green badge as magical as he from the paper bag. It might as well have been a genie in a lamp. I beamed. I'd created something from thin air that had sparked a reaction in my teacher and the feeling was incredible. As Maya Angelou said, 'People will forget what you did. But people will never forget how you made them feel.' And the feeling is as real today as it was 30 years ago, because in that exchange lay an early clue to my purpose as a storyteller – a woman with a message.

It is these moments where we experience elation that we must spend our life creating. Where our creativity lights us up from the inside out, and our light shines so brightly that we spark inspiration and joy in others. I didn't know that then, of course. I was seven. And 30 years later every written word I commit to this page feels just like blue cheese and black grapes. Delicious – and I relish the experience.

We cannot know where the road will lead and we mustn't get hung up on the destination, for to make the end goal our focus is to trivialize the richness of the journey. Surrender the grip on the steering wheel of your life. Step away from the driver's seat. Suspend the doubts and cynicism of the world, and embark on your own personal journey inwards to know yourself. And in knowing yourself revealing your oneness with all that is.

There's an infinite well of greatness within you, a capacity to co-create and transform your life, which will raise the roof off the possibilities for your existence if you're willing to hack away at your layers. Broken open by grief, in the living room of my parents' fifth-floor flat, I glimpsed the purest potential for who I am, who we all are.

This book flowed out of that miracle and I will forever be humbled by the process, which has been far from linear. As ambitious and driven as ever, my work ethic remains potent, but today I allow my relationship with the source to guide the direction of my life, rather than forcing or being attached to outcomes. Without my old relentless focus on attaining and accruing to achieve a predetermined goal, I'm free to create, unhampered and unrestricted by the attachment to output. I can marvel at the partners, collaborations and ideas that flow to me effortlessly thick and fast as I sail downstream, basking in the natural rhythm of the waters. Tuned into the stream of my own wellbeing – doing what feels good! I'm in complete alignment. I find myself entirely in my flow, and so I attract more of what is good and right and meant. That is the recipe for purpose-driven work.

Today, my own inner truth has replaced the lighthouse in my life that my dad once was and with its light always in view it's impossible not to be filled with awe. And as I breathe life into my better qualities and talents, picking myself up and dusting myself off each time I sink back into fear and old debilitating habits and views, success and abundance flow.

Today, more than ever before, I know my reason for being on this planet: to be the change. And whether it's simply seeking to leave the individuals I interact with each day feeling lifted and empowered or to change the whole world, the magnitude of my impact is almost irrelevant. It all starts with changing myself.

The likelihood is that your parents' experience wasn't one that allowed them the privilege of looking in at the disparity and separatist belief systems that govern our world with the enquiring eye that our generation is developing. For many of our parents, the mission was simply survival. For all of their toil, it's our obligation to lift the conversation higher. To live in a way where we look beyond the external casing both of ourselves and of others, and trust the soul of one another.

That girl who in childhood decided she must protect herself in an uncertain world, prove her worth, then fix her broken edges, is no longer me. Who I am, who we all are at our core, is love.

And when the world and its unconscious status quo cause you to retract from your newfound serenity and power, commit to returning to a state of gratitude even and particularly when life is at its toughest. Be thankful even, for being able to contemplate your purpose. Start each day with intent and remind yourself that you have a mission. And that support of the highest power is accessible to you as long as you make yourself open and available to receive it. There's nothing to fear, for fear itself is a construct of minds raised in a fear-driven world. You know better.

Stripped back and connected is where we meet ourselves. And from that place of exposure, our true purpose, the calling that dwells within us all, will be revealed. You picked up this book for a reason and whatever resonates is your call to action to explore. Leap off the cliff. The rest will unfold as it's meant. You only need to show up for the guidance, commit to the journey with all its varied textures and marvel as the miracles begin to appear in your purpose-driven life.

2020

*'And one day, unannounced, you begin to
feel your plants in their glossy ceramic pots,
silently crying out to be rooted into the earth.*

*And recognize within their call, your own
soul's desperate yearning to be rooted,
reconnected, returned... free of your own
glossy contained existence, to bloom.*

And truly you have no option but to listen.'

JESSICA HUIE

Four years on I now see with hindsight, that moment when my life was plunged into presence at the bedside of my father was just the start of a deeper unravelling.

Truth, in a cloak of beautiful, powerful black, was making her entrance. The Brexit verdict had felt shocking to me then. Frightening even. The politics and polarizing views had burst on to the scene at a moment in time when I found my heart at its most open. Made naked by grief.

There was no longer a place to hide. No matter how liberal, progressive or activated our little corners of community were, we were suddenly privy to the beliefs and values of the nation. It was a truth we'd all felt and been impacted by, but, in England, it became audible on the radio stations, social media platforms and in black taxi conversations. A humanity deeply polarized and divided.

Weeks after I was privileged to experience my father's spirit depart his physical form, Donald Trump would be made President of the United States. I cried, as did many.

We couldn't have known, then, that it was just the start of the age of uprising and reclamation that we all now bear witness to. Elephants in their droves, freed from their silent existence, now roaming free. And as the world clamoured to be heard, to resist change, reconcile or reclaim in equal proportion, the collective awakening triggered us all into confrontation with ourselves and our complicity. Many burrowed deep into the numbing comfort of their own denial and dissociation. Some were desperate to cling to the reigns of their power and control, others were catapulted into sharp, raw acknowledgement of the parts of ourselves we'd suppressed or compromised in order to survive. There was rage, fear, shame and in amongst the swamp of human emotion, the light, bright flickering of hope that this was the crisis preceding a collective raising of consciousness – a new way.

We were all hurtled into the stark truth of where we were as a global people. The plaster of complicity and apathy was ripped off our existence by a pandemic shrouded in contradiction.

The death of another black man, George Floyd, happened at a moment when the world was moving slowly enough to finally recognize the continued legacy of murder for the atrocity that it has always been and continues to be. The pounding clash of intersections cried out for congruence. It wasn't just racial harmony and equality that rose to the surface; a rebalancing of our very essence and relationship to the Earth also seemed called for, as well as an acknowledgement of who we really are.

The world was waking up. On my little Surrey street in the UK, as everything began to 'lockdown', it felt to me as though the walls were quite literally imploding. The box I suddenly had an acute awareness that I was paying to be occupant in, began to feel utterly claustrophobic. The feeling of suffocation had nothing to do with the size of our home. No, this strain on my metaphorical lungs was not Covid.

The strain was due to having existed within and subscribed to frameworks and ideologies that fundamentally conflicted with the very essence of our nature.

The dam was bursting and the thick collective energy of grief, fear and rage, particularly from within the black community, was piercing deeper layers of my own illusion.

And, my goodness, this time the breaking-open was physical. Energy coursed through my body with such ferocity that, during that spring of 2020, once my children were ensconced in their bedrooms, living room door closed, I'd spend night times, candles lit, dancing wildly as the sorrow and trauma that had been housed in my cells, and now surfaced, availed the opportunity to be released. The image is funny to me now. But I dug deeply into my spiritual practice, taking up chanting and an online Reiki course, and doubling down on my yoga asanas, meditation, journaling and daily walks in nature. Being a human felt so very painful, full of contradiction and out of alignment with truth to me, that anything that delivered me to that internal safe space within was a spiritual lifeline.

Deeper levels of my own aching conformity emerged: the many areas of my life in which I'd stuffed my true self down and complied. I had normalized an existence lived through the gaze of others – my parents, men, white people, black people, authority figures, institutions – so much so that I was blind to any other way of being. It all came up. All the areas in which I abandoned my Self – as in the truest, unchangeable, divine part of me, in pursuit of acceptance and belonging.

My tolerance for the disingenuous disappeared seemingly overnight. I recall one day returning from the daily ritual of a walk around the park and tearing down the rainbow in my window. My respect, support and appreciation of the NHS is unquestionable, but it was the superficiality of the ritual I could not and would no longer be party to. Several Thursdays I stood outside my door clapping the NHS healthcare workers working on the frontline of the Covid epidemic feeling conflicted, my soul bellowing, the facade of oneness so removed from my experience of the inequality that underpinned society. But the dots, then, hadn't fully connected. I was still submissively playing my 'role', the distinct feeling of superficiality about the ritual not yet risen close enough to my surface to be processed. And so there I stood, clapping like my inclusion depended on it. That was before George Floyd.

The skill of appeasing, pre-empting the needs and expectations of others before my own, was entrenched. The period of isolation enforced by the Covid virus was, for so, so many of us, the most almighty trigger into deeper awakening, exploding open the areas where we had been suppressing our truth. Compartmentalizing ourselves. 'Smalling up' just to exist. Leaving pieces of us and our truth parked away in corners whenever we sensed they might not be welcomed and agreeable.

And so it was that in April, just days after my 40th-birthday Zoom party, Spirit, in the form of a mid-afternoon meltdown, blasted through me with the clearest of guidance. 'Prepare to Leave' was the message. And so, 16 weeks later, on the very first flight out of the UK to Jamaica once borders had reopened (joined a fortnight later by my eight-year-old son), I did. For it is always this way when we say YES to our calling. So often we want to know how the plan for our lives will unfold before we make the leap, but, alas, it doesn't work that way. It is only when we can summon the chutzpah and courage to fall back into nothingness, bereft of a life jacket, that the Almighty's net appears to catch our fall and lift us, to raise us into a level of being that is only attainable from the mouth of surrender. Say yes and take a step, and we find the universe meeting us – with oceans of grace beyond comprehension, and a plan for our lives far more magnificent than anything we might strategize with our limited-thinking mind – exactly where we are.

I speak so much about honouring and saying yes to your calling. Indeed it is the crux of all that I stand for and share. We must make ourselves available to hear what it is that we need as those needs evolve, in honour of becoming the person life coaxes us into being. This 'saying yes' is motivated by the necessity for our own growth, evolution and becoming.

The other crucial part of that transformation is, however, letting go. Releasing that which ceases to align with our being as life's cocoon changes us. And that is by no means always easy.

Our internal changes call us to confront, heal and let go of beliefs and habits that keep us smaller than the truth of our greatness. As we work to return to the essence of who we were before all the 'stuff' tainted our glow, revelations and realizations will inevitably colour the call to make changes in our life. We have to accept what we need to release in order to allow space for who we need to become and the newness life wants to create through us.

It is rarely easy. Sometimes it's a job or career choice that no longer tees up with our soul's purpose. A friendship or social circle that is no longer conducive to our authentic peace.

I speak as somebody who grappled with the reality that I made vows in the full faith that I felt at that time in my life, to be married forever. Vows that society and the law says are binding. And I changed. Transformed, in fact. When I woke up through the passing of my dad, it became impossible to un-see. I was no longer the same woman who had made those vows.

Many of the things that I'd held up as important and defining to the being I was, were no longer. My soul needed different things. From the content of conversations to the dreams and ambitions that felt real to me, mine was a new hunger. And it was not at all about my partner not having been enough, only that our union no longer felt accurate to me, at least in the form of a marriage. What began as an integrity gap, between who I was being and who I needed to evolve into, soon became a crevice. A crack that was felt not just by me, but by all within our atmosphere and that did no justice to either of us or to our family.

And this is where the world of 'should' steps into the ring to face-off with what our measure of personal integrity knows to be true.

It's less about what is 'right' or 'wrong', and much more to do with the feeling of peace and congruence that is present when we occupy a space of unification and honour with our spirit's own gospel.

I made the decision to have that gospel be the only manual that would inform my life choices some time ago. I say 'made the decision' but the reality is that to let anything outside of myself dictate my decisions is too painful an internal conflict to bear and at odds with all that I stand for. It's a bold stand. But as we take up this mantle we discover that the choices that align with our own truth are always also in the highest interest of everyone else. That they may not always be able to see that at the time calls for compassionate understanding.

The grace and nobility with which my former husband and I were able to release one another from our marriage remains something I will forever be both proud of and humbled by. It is testament to what is possible from a place of pure love, when the need to be right, to judge or to blame is moved aside in place of a mutual commitment and desire for collective goodness and peace to prevail. Of course there were moments of conflict, hurt and dismay, the prospect of relinquishing our life together, even with its discord, in moments more appealing than the blank canvas of the unknown that separation signalled.

'Go and be happy,' he told me in a message before I left for Jamaica. Putting the future we had planned and aspired to behind us. It was, it strikes me now, perhaps the most unconditional illustration of love to frame our marriage. Ironic, then, that it was delivered in the goodbye.

And so a life in Jamaica beckoned. As I said 'yes' to the call, the presumed obstacles to stepping forward on to my heart and soul's path dissipated like clouds moved by miracles at the hand of God herself. A trail cushioned and guided my exit out of the UK and – more deeply than ever, through the layers of armour and passages of memories unchartered – into myself.

Stripped Back Is Where We Meet Ourselves

'I've realized that I need to be moved. To feel joy, to experience awe, to have my thoughts provoked, my senses stimulated, to be reduced to nothing but the moment, as often as possible. I don't care if it hurts. Let me feel. Just so I know I'm truly alive.'

JESSICA HUIE

I'm listening to the waves lapping outside my bedroom window, the cockerel signalling his morning call and the sound of the week-old kitten we rescued (when he fell off a wall and became family) clawing at the door for his breakfast. In no way, shape or form do I recognize my life.

It still feels surreal. I think about how, almost instantly, everything can change. Just like that, the life you recognize can be transformed into a completely alternative reality. That idea can unsettle or inspire you – depending on the window you choose to view it through.

For me, the possibilities that this knowing presents are exhilarating. We can see our ability to co-create our lives in high definition and in real-time. It isn't just the fact that seemingly overnight I went from feeling such a sense of confinement to watching my son in our swimming pool against the backdrop of the Caribbean sea, it's that the decision to move to Jamaica might just have been my bravest, realest, most conscious life choice ever.

The first big choice of my soul. A choice made not from a space of fear or conditioning, but from clarity. From being so in touch and awake to what felt good for me, and what did not, and choosing to act in the direction of that goodness, despite the fear of the many, many unknowns. Finally, *finally* I had become available both to listen to and hear myself. For we can only access the counsel of our divine guides once we have reconnected to ourselves intimately.

How often do we just land in places – manage to arrive in relationships, careers, the places we live, the lifestyles we uphold, for reasons other than pure intention? How often do we really and truly *choose*? I'm not talking about the kind of choices that are in themselves a product of somebody else's ideology, unconscious trauma or a kind of sleep-walking habit. When was the last time that you had the presence to consciously connect with your ultimate vision for your existence and choose it all?

The smells... for me it's ylang ylang, frankincense and lavender on the burner mixed with the natural scent of the tropics. Blue mountain coffee with all its rich layers in my cup.

The sights... just ocean and palms, greens and turquoises. My kids in the pool, my friends talking late into the night over a bottle of white wine that's crisp and chilled in the fridge.

The sounds... the water lapping, my wind chime made magic by the breeze.

The tastes... coconut water, mangoes for eons and roasted breadfruit.

And the feel... Cloth as loose as possible on my body. Toes liberated to wiggle free of socks, the kiss of the sun on my skin, a slow, steady breath now. Distanced from the adrenaline-motored existence that I overdosed on, operating within the epicentre of the machine, until I slowly began to wake...

I visualized it all. Meditated on it. And well before I thought I was ready, the call came to leap and my only task was to say 'yes', without clarity around the *how*; oh, and perhaps most importantly, to be willing to let go of what no longer aligned with me. Over and over again we'll be presented with opportunities to level up mind, body and spirit. I don't think the fear ever goes away when stepping into the unknown. But in recognizing our fear as a signal, we are moving into sacred territory where we are closing the integrity gap between the life our soul desires and the one that we are living; we can go forward in full faith that we are held.

We always have so many more choices than we realize...

Our potential to create change and actualize our dreams is only as possible as our recognition and belief in our own power to do so.

And I was certainly only able to make this choice of a move across the world, to know that it was even available to me, and to be in touch with how I felt in Jamaica, because of the unstripping that had begun to occur in earnest after dad passed on – the beautiful dawn that grief presents. All of that 'work,' near ten years of trying (rather than allowing) healing, and I now see that I had just been getting started. For the irony is that, while nothing will change the huge love and adoration I hold for my father, being released – at least in the physical sense – from my strong identification with the role of being his daughter, left all of my roles, and every patch in the patchwork of my identity, up for questioning and exploration.

After writing the first edition of *Purpose*, success became purely about freedom. The freedom to discover and embody all of me. It came thick and fast, so much so that it destabilized my world. The life I'd thought I wanted revealed itself as one that had become out of alignment with the light inside me, which was becoming increasingly bright and loud. The light refused to be silenced, irrespective of whether its unveiling caused momentary chaos in its wake.

It had been silenced too long. The legacy of a childhood in which, like so many second-generation immigrants and children of post-war parents can attest, the expression of feelings was unwelcome. My feelings, in the wake of parents who were not afforded the benefits of space and resources to explore and heal their *own* trauma, were so painful and potent that I learned to squash them down into my little body and dissociate through a multitude of ways.

So when I broke open, my feelings came flooding out with such velocity, I sometimes feared they would wash me away. Feeling your feelings, it turns out, can be terrifyingly hard to do. The hardest thing to do. And what a shock it was to discover how much had been buried. Locked into the cells of my being.

Yes, there were many difficult nights – lonely, painful but brave nights where I would no longer run from what needed to surface and be set free. After Dad passed on, I committed to my healing as though my life depended on it. In many ways it did. Stemming the tide of trauma's inter-generational legacy became my priority above all else.

Yes, freedom – from the imprisonment of mental enslavement, from the shackles of historic pain, from any residual feelings of unworthiness that stood as obstacles to the creation of a life more beautiful, joyous and purposeful than I could fathom – became the only measure of success that felt real for me.

As I began to experience deeper degrees of healing, the light within me began to shine brighter and my relationship with cultivating it strengthened. I learned how and when it shone most exuberantly, where and why it felt lit up. Until one day, without announcement, I came to recognize *myself* as this light, this holy being – no longer just conceptually but actually, with much more ease and identification than anything external.

One of my favourite-ever quotes is by Marianne Williamson: 'You are only beholden to the values of the paradigm you subscribe to.' Quite. And that is exactly what occurs when you embark on this journey back home to becoming your true Self. As your identification with who you are shifts, all is up for questioning. Day by day, if we stay on the path with faith and connection as our anchors, freedom from trauma, freedom from systemic oppression, freedom from limiting beliefs and stories, freedom from separation and false notions of love, will all become our birthright. But there is no way around the marshes. Standing in the centre of the fire changes you. If we are courageous enough to venture deep down and far away from the light, we can also soar to heights of equal proportion.

About two months after moving to Jamaica I was taking a walk one morning before I began my day and was hit by a flashback. I'd been eight years old and spending the school summer holiday in Jamaica with my family and we had driven past the housing development where I now lived, probably en route to the beach. From the back of the car, the houses, all different in their architecture and framed by mighty palms with glints of turquoise pools in some cases, had captivated me. *'One day,'* I'd thought, *I'm going to live in a house just like that right by the sea.* The memory of that conscious thought was visceral and hit me like a lightbulb. The house we now occupied had been one of only three that an estate-agent friend of the family, Maura, had sent to me via WhatsApp and included a short video of the outside view. The house itself was simple and basic, missing the mod cons of my UK lifestyle, but I was unphased. Something inside of me whispered that the simplicity might present exactly the space I needed and an opportunity for a life unhampered by convenience. A return to basics. An invitation to find again the gift in the presence that washing a coffee mug can deliver; being present enough to actually experience the feel of water on my skin. To just *be here now*.

As it happens, as a single working mother, I would soon discover that a balance between my idealized perception of country life and cosmopolitan city existence was more suited and realistic for the pursuit of my creative goals. This included my work with The Purpose Academy, supporting the many individuals who join each year to breathe life into their own projects and businesses. But, in many ways, I realized that less was more. I was reminded that the sweet spot in a life of alignment is where we choose what we desire, rather than *needing* things in order to be. It was a powerful reminder of what is real and important.

In retrospect, I was undergoing a process of purification. So much was coming to the surface about my womanhood and relationships and where my choices had unconsciously been fuelled by fear and lack, rather than love. Choices created and perpetuated by the narratives that value completion via somebody or something outside of ourselves. That dynamic can never be sustainable without a huge compromise of the self.

It was almost as though, having placed my flag in the ground for 'purpose', the universe said, *Now live it.*

In the quiet of those many early nights, when the sun would set over the sea outside of my window in a blaze of golden glory each evening, and mosquito hour (between 6 p.m. and 7-ish, in case you ever feel called to visit the Caribbean or sign up to my annual Purpose Retreat) signalled a snuggle and chapter of reading with my son before lights out, there was certainly loneliness, and dark, confronting times. Times when the sounds were alien and the life unknown and the future so unpromised, but within all of that, deep down, a peace. The path of purpose can at times be a lonely one. No matter how extensive our network and friendship circles are, we must venture into spaces within ourselves where we alone can dwell and be with ourselves uncompromisingly. Whatever we find. We must learn to hold our fractured pieces and love them back together.

Take heart though. For the reward for our courage, in returning to the pure essence of love that we are, is the doorway to bliss.

Beyond Judgement

*'If we knew today what we will know tomorrow,
perhaps we would cling less tightly to the need
to control and drive outcomes. We would exhale.
Trust. Accept.*

*For if we knew today what life will reveal
tomorrow, we would see that everything is
indeed unfolding in delectable, divine order.'*

JESSICA HUIE

Some months into our new life in Jamaica it was decided that my son would return to the UK for Christmas to spend time with family. The plan was that I would join him after a fortnight, spend a week in the UK, and then return to Jamaica with my little boy. What actually occurred, as a result of the pandemic's impact on our ability to travel, was that my flight was cancelled and we found ourselves separated for nearly two months. At least I knew he was safe and happy with his father in the UK.

Needless to say, initially I was grateful for the mum break and the space and time to flow. But as the weeks went on, without a clear plan as to how or when I might be able to reunite with him, I became increasingly angsty.

Knowing and trusting that everything that unfolds in our lives is for our evolution is one thing, but remembering and returning to that principle in the thick of the quagmire is where the mettle of our core, the strength of our faith, is put to the test.

I now recognize that the events that played out one after the other during those two months, when I was availed the space to process and integrate them, were all a part of God's plan.

Jamaica is brimming over with creativity and entrepreneurship at every level, from the vendors who'll attempt to wash your windscreen whilst you sit at the traffic lights and the women braiding tourists' hair at the beach, to the culture-shaping icons who have impacted the entire world through art, politics, food, music and more. Having been pretty much grounded by adjusting to life in the country and running the Academy, I began to feel hungry to connect with the many inspiring, creative small-business owners who were crossing my path and to explore opportunities to support and collaborate through the sharing of my own gifts. And so it was that, with the help of a wonderful Kingston-based fashion stylist named Kaysian Bourke, aka 'Flowerchild', I invited a small group of micro- and small-biz owners and creatives to convene in the front yard of a little art gallery in Kingston.

My agenda? Simply to explore what magic the drive I'd felt, to bring a group of women together, might reveal. As we worked our way around the circle of women sitting outside the gallery,

I felt high from the connection that occurs when goddesses commune. Boundaries dropped away as we all shared an insight into our work and how we had arrived at what it is that we do today.

The journey of these women both broke my heart and healed it simultaneously. As I listened, the thread – which appears to me in my mind's eye as red in colour and silken in texture – binding and connecting our individual and collective journeys, began to reveal itself. For beneath the personal stories of women now singing, styling or running a small fashion brand for a living, was this unified story of beings deeply passionate about the land that was their, and now my, home. Way beyond their own desire to achieve their personal vision of success, was this reverence for Jamaica. A reverence and commitment to uplifting the country that had broken them open and continued to feed and inspire their souls, in equal measure.

When Zia Benjamin spoke, the silence was palpable.

'I chose to come back to Jamaica. It wasn't something I had to do, I was called back to this place to do the shadow work,' said Zia.

It was Flowerchild that introduced me to Zia, quite early into my time bedding down into life in Jamaica. Several people in isolation had suggested we'd get along so well and so on New Year's Eve of 2020, with my son away in London, I met this star soul for dinner at House Boat Grill in Montego Bay. It's a restaurant on a stationary boat on the water and it's yummy – do visit.

Beautiful in the realest way, Zia's effervescence flows from her grace and her kind and gentle soul. It was our first meeting, but my heart knew hers.

One of Jamaica's leading female singers, she's an exciting presence on a music scene that is evolving as the culture does. She is questioning and pushing the boundaries, breaking down the boxes that have too long dictated what musical artistry means for women from the island who achieve a level of success in the entertainment industry.

Zia, like anyone committed to living their purpose, is dedicated to unapologetically being who she is, and her Rum Shop Blues vibe is captivating.

Life offers up the experiences, however crippling, that are most beneficial to the expansion of our soul. When we can reach and touch a state of grace and, better still, a gratitude for the wisdom and healing gleaned from the hardest events in our lives, we transform.

Zia was a teenager and at a friend's house after a party in Jamaica's capital city, when she received the phone call that was to bookend one chapter of her life and signal the start of another. On the end of the phone line was her mother explaining in words that Zia could not yet fully comprehend, that her father had been killed by a group of 17-year-olds. The day before, she and her father had argued in the way that teens inevitably will clash with their parents as they traverse that bumpy terrain between child- and adulthood.

The crime rate in Jamaica is something that has long been the focus of the media's narrative around the island. It's often sensationalized and so I tread sensitively lest I do anything to perpetuate that narrative. I would not have upped sticks and moved to the island with my son had I not felt it was safe for us to dwell here. But the fact remains that where there is economic disparity and unrest, crime will exist. Things have much improved but there remains work to do. Jamaica remains a place that everyone should visit in their lifetime. It is unlike anywhere else on Earth, so true in its loyalty to its own original essence.

'This country, which I love still, completely broke me. The pain of losing my dad, it shattered me. But sometimes breaking open can really force you to grow and expand. It gives you real empathy, and a sense that life, however transient, should have meaning and purpose. I will never be the person I was, but in my journey of healing I've learned to fill the cracks with molten gold, hope, fire to be reborn and help others on their healing journeys. Sometimes you have to make beauty out of breaking.'

It was music that revealed itself as both Zia's healing and her calling: 'Music is a thing that forces you to look in the mirror and question yourself at every single turn. Every single lyric, if it comes from the heart, is shadow work. I think everyone has their calling and most of the time that is terrifying. If it inspires you, but scares you, it's probably the direction you should head in because that's how we grow: by channelling our inspirations and challenging our fears.'

She continued, 'I feel strongly that Jamaica occupies some kind of a vortex because for better or for worse we are all operating with some kind of potent, higher energy and that's why everybody is so creative. The man on the corner selling coconuts is a healer and a wise man. The woman selling panties on the roadside can sing your face off. Everyone is a star in Jamaica. So for me, for a time, that opened up doubt and questioning as to whether my voice was necessary and valid. My music became my healing and I was terrified to release it because it was so personal... but that is where purpose comes into play.'

The decision to allow our voice to be heard, to reveal ourselves in all of our messy realness and live our truth, although scary, seems to me the greatest act of devotion and revolution, both for ourselves and the source from which we emanate.

For years Zia's music remained her personal secret as she locked the trauma from the loss of her father into her deepest, darkest corners and threw herself into work. A talented journalism student, she began creating documentaries about how to deal with grief, interviewing people going through the process and intellectualizing her own pain in the process. She spoke with refugees from Sudan, including a former child soldier who was trying to reclaim his life after being forced to kill his entire family. She interviewed Holocaust survivors and those who had lost the loves of their life. She studied genocide survivors to understand how countries who have been through the worst kind of atrocity were able to still find peace and move forward. As she explains it, Zia shoved her humanity, her own pain, to the back and tried to understand grief and altruism and what it takes for a person to lose their humanity and then regain it. She hurtled into work as though her sanity depended on it, finding solace and distraction from her own grief by being a compassionate ear and mouthpiece for others – which in itself is God's work, right? Except that there comes a time when being of service can become just another way in which we avoid feeling that which cries out to us, in the name of our own recovery, to be processed and felt.

Zia said: 'Even in that period of my life, I felt like the microphone. It was important for me to amplify these voices, but I wasn't facing myself. It was music and poetry that brought me back to me. And that's why it's so terrifying to be that honest and then share the work, and if it's not honest you can't sit with it, or really celebrate it, because you feel it in your bones when you're not creating with your truth. Honest creativity provides sanctuary, for yourself and others.

Once I started releasing my own music, people started to compare me to incredible, untouchable artists like Billie Holiday and Nina Simone, which was a shock and a blessing. But how do you live up to those comparisons? It's only recently that I realized you *don't* live up to those comparisons, you live up to being as true to yourself as possible and you stay open and allow creation to work through you to create something new. Comparison is just people putting you in a category so they can understand you – don't be too flattered, or too fearful of it. Your job is to be you, provide sanctuary with your truth, and even if just one person is impacted by something you share, that is everything. It doesn't need to be a million to matter.'

'How do you do the dance?', I asked Zia. For when you finally make that mighty and vulnerable transition into sharing your gifts with the world, they stem from your soul. And within the paradigm of a world that often prizes the output of the head above the heart, our spirit can inevitably feel conflicted. For while Zia recognizes on the realest level that success lies simply in her being her fully expressed, musically gifted self and blessing the world in her sharing, irrespective of any tools of measurement, the music industry, built on bricks of different value, says otherwise.

'The person that writes the songs? That is me, and that person is quite introverted, to be honest,' said Zia. 'When I think about the machine, I have to be a different person for that. It can make me feel hopeless, because I have to care about things I don't really care about to do well in this industry, but it's a necessary dance. I choose to get past my own discomfort around any feelings of conflict, because I know it's bigger than me. I speak at girls' schools, and I want to start a record label for girls someday, because when I started I had male producers telling me women don't "buss" out of Jamaica and so it doesn't make sense to record them. For that reason alone, I have to give my best to this. My visibility and voice, added to those of other female artists who are speaking or singing their truths, will help show young girls in Jamaica that they can be true to themselves. You don't have to fit into an easily marketable box; you can sell your soulfulness without selling-out your soul. As a female artist in Jamaica, you don't have to choose between the extremes of wearing batty-riders (hot pants) or a long, conservative dress and singing conscious reggae music to be acceptable. Not that those are bad – they are beautiful expressions of our culture – but there are other expressions ready to be birthed by this country. We and they can move beyond the limitations of culture and conditioning.

It's more important than a lot of people realize, because when a woman does well, if she is willing to bring her tribe, she can really bring them far. You are supporting the jewellers you wear, the fashion brands you wear. You are literally uplifting the economy of Jamaica just by showing up and doing well. Amplifying women's voices can change the country – any developing country – and so we do the dance. My father was such an incredible spirit and he used to call me a bright spark so I've really tried to be that for people. To encourage them to seek themselves, to journey within and find their own brightness and just share that.'

I love the light that is Zia Benjamin. She is just one of the gifts my life in Jamaica has delivered to me. You can share in her beautiful energy by finding @ziabenjamin on Instagram.

We moved around the circle, and for fashion designer and stylist Flowerchild, grief also revealed itself as a portal unlocking access to deeper and more expanded layers of her artistry and creations in the world. It liberated fathomless layers of herself...

Life delivered Flowerchild more loss before she turned thirty years old than many people experience in a lifetime. Aged 17, she watched her 15-year-old brother drown: 'I remember going back to school and sitting at the lunch table with all of the girls who were chatting about what they would wear at the weekend and I remember thinking, *I am no longer the same. I am changed.* Something had shifted.'

Later, Peter, the love of her life and father to her son, would lose his battle with cancer while she was at his side. Her sister would overdose on prescription pills, her one-year-old godson would walk into a swimming pool... so much loss. I was in awe of Flowerchild's grace and gentleness. This woman has such softness despite the magnitude of grief she has been bequeathed.

It was, however, the passing of her best friend and business partner Dexter '3D' Pottinger, whom the Jamaican press once described as 'our Galliano', that was the turning point at which her art – her purpose – became the thing that both released and saved her.

Aged 19, she'd started *First* magazine to showcase the richness of Caribbean culture. It began turning up on what she described as 'a lot of important people's coffee tables in New York and London'. Out of the blue, *Vanity Fair* contacted her, wanting to feature her work. 'I couldn't believe it and went running to the pharmacy to buy a copy of the magazine to see if the woman was a real journalist!'

She was passionate about attaching *First* magazine to philanthropy and the *Vanity Fair* exposure lead to Hewlett Packard contacting her out of the blue to donate 100 laptops to a children's home in Jamaica. 'I achieved a lot with that project. Everybody was on board for the love of it – we were a very poor magazine,' she laughs.

Dexter 3D Pottinger had been her best friend from school. He was dyslexic and she was a teacher's pet but they were both creatives and that was the thread that bound them. As early as nine years old they noticed each other's work:

'One year the cheerleading team came out in these booties. Dexter had got cartridge paper and cut them out like boots and whitened the paper, finding a way to attach them to the shoes. It was genius!' says Flowerchild.

Later they began working together and never left each other's side, until 2017, when he transcended. Dexter had helped her break into styling. She was a designer and, once she'd started the magazine, he would often not show up to style the photo shoots, so it nudged her into believing she could be a wardrobe stylist: 'He taught me how to push myself without saying too much, created scenarios that forced me to trust myself.' Independently they began styling the many foreign artists who would come to Jamaica, idyllic shoot backdrop and artistic hub that it is. They were always in the background supporting each other, Flowerchild at Dexter's house in the middle of the night asking, 'What do you think about this look?'

Dexter always used to say, 'Kaysian, if me get fi style Beyoncé it done!' That was his ultimate styling dream. Flowerchild shared what unfolded after Dexter passed on in 2017…

'I was going through a rough space, getting a divorce and I wasn't sure where I was with my career. I was raising my kids in Jamaica and there weren't that many international opportunities coming through the door. I could literally hear

Dexter on so many days saying "one foot in front of the other". One day I went and styled an artist and the producer was watching me, noticing that I was going above and beyond on set. I was sitting at a friend's house and they called me and said we have a project for you but you have to sign an NDA (non-disclosure agreement). I signed and sent it back. I drove home thinking, "Oh my gosh, I pray it's Solange!" My ultimate would have been styling Solange and his ultimate would have been Beyoncé. He had only recently died, just two months earlier.

At that time, all that kept going through my mind was how I was going to continue Dexter's legacy. I kept saying the word "legacy" to myself and to others.

I got home, opened the email and it said, Beyoncé, Jay-Z and the Carter twins – Legacy. Legacy was the name of the project. I cried for two hours straight. It was the On the Run tour. There was a head stylist, Zerina Akers, and I was to be her right hand – the eyes on the ground who knew Jamaican culture.

When I got to that project, people must have thought I was crazy because I was literally talking to Dexter the whole time saying, "This project is important to us!" I really wanted to make him proud. I really wasn't doing that project for just me. A lot of the blessings that came from it are because I put so much passion into it for him. Whatever I do now, I carry him under my wings because I know I am blessed enough to have the gift of breath within my body. I can't waste this opportunity. My creativity saved me.'

Following the shoot, Flowerchild gifted the team a package of Jamaican artisans' produce to illustrate that Jamaican designers can sit alongside creatives from the most cosmopolitan cities in the world. So often the artistry of islanders is excluded from the global narrative around fashion. Included in the package was Flowerchild's signature bag. A bag that Beyoncé would later spontaneously wear to Milan Fashion Week.

A little time after Dexter's passing, Flowerchild created a fashion show which would become one of the high points of her career and a landmark moment in her personal journey. *The Flower Widow* collection was art for the runway that expanded beyond the traditional boundaries of fashion, incorporating video and poetry and connecting with the audience so much that when they stood in standing ovation, they too wept with the designer who had channelled her own chasm of grief into beauty shared with the world, honouring Dexter 3D Pottinger, and life, with all of its stark polarities, in the process. Share in Flowerchild's journey @Originalflowerchild1999

I was moved by the stories I'd heard that day. Full of that beautiful and affirming sense that washes over you when you feel yourself viscerally in your flow, plugged into connection with source and the knowledge that none of our steps are ever walked alone.

We freshened up and headed out for a dinner in Kingston, laughing, jovial and feeling all of the deliciousness of sisterhood thanks to our nourishing circle.

At this point it feels pertinent to explain that we were yet to have so much as a glass of wine. Earlier that day, before our women's circle, I'd taken a blissful sojourn into Devon House (a must-visit for some of the world's best ice cream) and stopped at Rosie's Crystal Gallery, which proudly boasts of being the island's first and only store stocking crystals and educating on their use.

I'd felt drawn to moldavite, a powerful rock found in Germany, Austria and the Czech Republic, believed to have formed following a meteor crash about 15 million years ago. Its impact is said to have had more power than an atomic explosion, the stone being created by the heat from the force of the impact. I remembered that a wise friend had told me that moldavite is a stone that aids transformation. For whatever reason, that afternoon I'd selected the slate grey–green stone housed in a pendant, where it would rest close to my heart chakra to work its power. I was well aware that its vibration strongly stimulates the auric field – to the extent that many feel an intense heat when they hold or wear it. With this stone, my warning is to start slowly...

The events that followed just hours after I placed the pendant to my chest were to become the second time a crystal had seemed to synchronously support the ushering-in of a significant turning point in my life.

Months earlier, I'd sat in my car in the parking lot of my Surrey health club, where I'd headed weekly for yoga classes. That day, it was the most private place to speak with my friend and Hay House peer Yamile Yemoonyah, author of *The Seven Types of Spirit Guide*, who through her incredible gifts was giving me a reading. What she shared is both personal and sacred, but amidst her download were two particularly poignant reflections:

'Very soon, you are going to have a major lifestyle upgrade,' said Yamile.

Of course, it would be a matter of weeks before the pandemic hit and I'd decide to up sticks and move to an island – and, as I sat in the parking lot on a blustery but bright March day in Raynes Park, I had no idea what she was talking about. Later in the reading she advised me to get a green crystal and wear it close to my heart so it could stimulate and open the heart chakra. On this occasion I decided to let the crystal find me.

Less than a fortnight later, the pandemic would change all of our lives and I'd find myself in a health store in London's Brixton, stocking up on sea moss and black seed oil in an effort to boost my family's immune system. It's a wonderful treasure chest of a store and I'd been transfixed by a dreamcatcher hanging from the ceiling. 'Is it for sale?' I asked the store assistant, explaining I was keen to purchase it as an early present to myself for my 40th birthday the next week. The sweet man shared that it was a part of their display but because it was my birthday he was willing to let me have it for a nominal fee, and he'd also like to give me a gift. He disappeared into the back of the store and re-emerged with, you guessed it... a beautiful green calcite crystal. I smiled from the inside out in recognition of this sign. *I am divinely guided*, chimed the thought.

Back to Kingston, Jamaica, and looking forward to eating something yummy. The night sky was a deep indigo blue and the street was dimly lit. The sound of a bassline pierced the air from the speaker right across the road and, walking a few steps ahead of my girlfriends, I recall glancing up to try to gauge the name of the venue the music was pumping from.

And that's when I fell.

Tumbling, tumbling... that's how it felt. Like I was Alice hurtling down Wonderland's rabbit hole, as though, just for a few milliseconds, which felt more akin to minutes, I was outside of time and space. Just a silent, sound-less, thought-less falling. There was a peace even. A calm within the nothingness. A freedom from thinking and identification. It was an uninitiated, spontaneous surrender.

As I landed in the open trench in the road, probably eight foot in depth and four foot wide, my mind kicked back in and with it came fear, bringing the serene, silent calm to an abrupt end. The thoughts flashed in quick succession: *'Am I dead? What if I can't get out? What might be in here! Rats? Infestation?'* It was one of the most terrifying experiences I've had.

Of course my sense of time was skewed but the memory of raising my head to look up in an attempt to gauge how far away safety, normality – my life – was is imprinted in high definition.

Intuition tells me that the memory of the switch from no thought back to thought – which slowed down so much that I was able to observe it from outside of myself – has something to teach me. I took one glance up at the gaping entrance left uncovered on the pavement, and suddenly several men, two, three or four, I have no idea, were present in the trench with me, and the relief at their reassuring words and hands lifting my legs back up, towards the faint light at street level, opened the floodgates to my tears.

Shock robbed me of words. But I know my friends Emma and Sydney, who were waiting to embrace me, will have thanked the men kindly for leaping so immediately to recover me.

The next couple of hours are something of a blur. I'd landed like a cat, my hand and foot breaking my fall. I was thankfully unscathed aside from cuts to my foot and shins and a very painful and increasingly purple finger, which I feared broken. Ice, alcohol to clean the wounds and plasters appeared. There was a silent dinner and a glass of red wine and then I was back at my hotel. I closed the door on my friends and enjoyed the comforting heat of the shower, where my tears joined with the water beating against my skin, and then I found the sanctuary of the bed.

Everything happens for us. That night juxtaposed alongside an afternoon that had felt holy – as, for me, divinity resides in connection. What is spirituality if not oneness? Yes, the night was one of little sleep. My sobs fell as though the stream might never end and I found myself back in the blackness of a hole, but this time, at least until the morning, completely alone with myself in a metaphorical trench of voluntary unconstrained grieving, which was utterly healing. I'm blessed to have loving friends all over the world, but in that moment there was nobody to call and it was an aloneness and disconnection from nurture I'd known before; a wholly familiar sense of the necessity to hold myself, which was so old and so frightening to confront that I'd buried it deep into my unconscious. That night, life nudged me into finally feeling it.

I cannot claim to understand the instance in its entirety, at least not on a conscious level, but I'm not sure that is the point. I accept that our wisdom is multidimensional and availed to us all in the good time we are prepared and available for it. But there is no question in my mind that the fall had put me in touch with a pain that had felt previously unreachable. I was blocked from my connection to feel and transmute it by numbing. Life, that night, gifted me a shaking that even I, with all of my control and competence, could not withstand. When the sun rose, something had finally been felt, shifted and cleared.

The next evening, with one foot still in the realm of the ethereal, having spent the day in the local hospital – where my swollen, purple finger's X-ray revealed not a breakage at all but ligament damage – I sat up in the hills of Kingston, eager to immerse myself in beauty again after the events of the night before.

I'd been broken open again by the trench experience and the unworldly night that had followed it, and yet that cracking open had left me feeling deeply connected. So much so that there, drinking in the mountain views, I fell in love with the earth more deeply then ever. Needless to say, I'm a proud second-generation Jamaican, and my love for the country had meant I'd been back twice a year for most of my adult life, but this love was different.

It was after an evening of dancing and vibing in amongst the cradle of nature. Walls of green palms, a ceiling made of stars, and a view of what seemed to be the entire land of Xamayca – 'the land of wood and water' – as it was once named by the island's indigenous Taino people, before it became Jamaica. The scent of sage and ganja whistling through and cleansing the air as spirits mingled and occupied their own space simultaneously. Yeah, dub club is a vibe.

High on sweet oneness, my friends and I wandered back to the car, taking a moment just to sit in silent wonder and drink in the panorama. And that's when I felt it. This tsunami of love for the land with its potent energy. Not just its divine beauty but its raw pain. Jamaica, it struck me in that moment, contains within it the entirety of our universal experience. Perhaps part of its magnetism, felt by all who touch its shores, is that the plaster, the buffer of the superficial – so much of the distraction and layering that defines Western culture and shields, distracts and disconnects us from our truth – is absent in the culture of the island. While the reality is that it is neither, it can initially feel like both the gift and the curse for those unattuned to its naked purity.

Jamaica doesn't have the window dressing and false sense of security provided by everything from health and safety protocols (see previous trench-fall experience) 'Uber' convenience culture to entire geographic areas devoted to feeding materialism and in turn upholding the unspoken call to look outside, rather than within, for meaning.

Without the plasters, you get to actually *feel* what is real. What I'm reminded of, right here, right now, as I write and share this, returning me to the moments when so much of who I was died with my father whilst his hand nestled in mine, is that stripped-back is where we meet ourselves.

While there are certainly strong arguments for both real and metaphorical open trenches being covered and potholes in the road being filled, the opportunity to get in touch with both the beauty of paradise and all of its abundance of aliveness – the music, the nature, the celebration of life at every step you take – *and* the juxtaposition of death, grief, pain in such close proximity, all of which Jamaica encapsulates, is a chance to accept, find peace and integrate it all.

To meet ourselves exactly where we are in an act of radical, compassionate self-acceptance is where the fight with ourselves begins to end.

When we start to let go of the lofty and rigid standards and rules that keep us in a state of perfectionism and perpetual internal chiding, everything begins to soften. Our entire being is availed the opportunity to dance in the fullness of our self-expression.

No good days, no bad days, just days... and all is welcomed and honoured just as it is. For it is *all* perfect. And in that revelation, we exhale. We move beyond judgement and attachment to any of it, to anyone or anything, and embrace all of what it means to be alive. In that sweet acceptance of all it means, we can awaken to and embrace all of the facets of ourselves. All of the parts of ourselves – the shame, the trauma we swept away but that was left lingering in our bodies at a cellular level: we can feel and embrace it all so it might no longer silently shackle and define us, for it is not all of us.

When we leave judgement and rejection behind, we can open our arms, perhaps for the first time ever, to every single part of us, and loving, ravishing ourselves with a fervour and appreciation of the gods and goddesses that we are. As we release both our judgement and propensity to control the outcomes of the experiences in our lives, we create the space for connection to the infinite generosity and support of the universe. We leave space for God's greater plan for our lives – the one bigger and higher than our own agenda – to reign.

When we release our tight grip around all that is, and we free ourselves from the crushing boxes we make ourselves squeeze into and conform to, we leave space for a curious heart and mind, one that considers the possibility that all that is unfolding in our lives is exactly as it should be and that there is an intelligence within it all, and we can shift into a new frequency of existing.

This personal version of the awakened new capacity to love all of ourself and our journeys, however arduous, painful and blessed, found me sitting way up in the hills at midnight, breath taken away by the vista on one unforgettable night in Kingston. However, while Jamaica holds its unique magnetism and magic, the eruption within your heart may strike and lift you anywhere – when the division between you and the earth itself liquefies and suddenly we can see and know our reflection in the moon. Watch the wind move the leaves of a tree and recognize our own lung's breath as no different. Recognize our own ancestral legacy as the roots from the oak unshakeable and fixed deep into the earth. No longer appreciating nature as something *outside* of ourselves, but feeling our oneness as a part of it.

In the space of 36 hours, I'd gone from the nurture and sanctified connection of our women's circle, to finding myself having fallen into a hole beneath ground level. Life had delivered me extreme experiences of the only two states of being in the language of the soul – fear and love. A profound reminder that we are only ever – if we probe into every thought and action we take – driven by one of those two frequencies. One that clings to all that we have, seeking to grasp and attack, the other that expands, opens, soothes and shares. *Which* frequency we decide to have guide our life, and be the crayon with which our existence is created, rests in the quality of our awareness and intention.

I was overcome with presence to the feeling of being pure love, and *in* love. A much, much deeper and all-encompassing capacity for love than I had ever known, enraptured with the land on which my feet had become entwined and beyond, with a quiet, blissful awareness that this was a healing – a healing I had been called to the country of one side of my ancestry to allow. And though it had terrified and implored me to make a leap and leave behind the life I'd worked so hard to create, I'd listened.

And that night, up in the hills with my girlfriends Emma and Sydney beside me, yet immersed in their own silent wonder,

for me the stars, perhaps each one an ancestor looking down
with a knowing smile, had never sparkled so brightly.

Rise in Love

'And just by being you,
I have become more me than I have ever been.'

Jessica Huie

Nine days after my trench experience, driving back to the countryside from our weekend in Kingston, I was to discover what becomes possible when we find ourselves opened up to this wholesome capacity to love, this raw recognition that we are beneath the costumes of our bodies. That love appeared in the vehicle of a meeting with a being whose own energetic frequency was siphoning through the cosmos towards me, matching my own.

For it is always that way, our internal experience and vibration always perfectly attracting the experiences and people most resonant and beneficial to the evolution of our soul at any given moment – even, in fact especially, when we aren't consciously looking for them.

The beauty of this meeting was the completely unassuming nature of it. I was still absorbing my adventures in Kingston, basking in what it means to sweep up all of the parts of ourselves and bring them home into ourselves and unquestionably emanate that knowing... I was vibing high.

My heart, now more open than ever before, had created an opening for nothing but more love to be ushered unto myself. It was now, I recognize, an inevitability. I had *become* (at least for a time, for I'm utterly human) that which I most deeply desired. And so it was that an evening that promised an agenda unknown to me, on any conscious level, delivered an introduction into the rest of my life.

'Just by being you,' he said, 'I have become more me than I have ever been.' In the bliss of an evening's interaction birthed from being our authentic selves, with talk of what we *do* parked in place for a sharing of who we *are*, we didn't so much 'fall', but rose, in love. Just as in that sacred, honest vortex that I'd discovered seated beside my father as he transcended, time melted beyond boundaries and we found ourselves home, plunged into truth.

We were vulnerable, open, real and fully surrendered to the magic that unfolded from that evening, and that remains as I write these words today, a connection as pure as it began.

It is not just a connection bound by the two of us, but a recognition of the divinity our harmony could represent, *must* represent, if it was to uphold the sanctity of the purpose it promised. A reminder here that purpose for me does not carry heavy notions of responsibility; on the contrary, it's about a return to simply being love, and the ripple effect that *being* catalyses.

Just as we can live with the intention to have all that stands before our true self-expression in the world fall away so we might be the change, in our union we sensed that we'd been brought together and bonded by something bigger than us, for a dual purpose. This purpose isn't born of intellect or role modelling or anything as surface-level as perception, but a purpose far bigger and more beautiful: to have our relationship be a tapestry woven from the thread of truth, of continued vulnerability and unconditional love, to see ourselves and each other truly, and to live and cultivate a love from that space.

With that purpose, our connection, just by granting it the permission and space to flourish with source as its unapologetic foundation, would be of service in the world. Without having to *do* a thing.

The grace of that recognition, for me, delivered via a series of the perfect challenges, highs, heartbreaks, wins and one meeting on a low-key evening, still takes my breath away. It's a return to a love unlike any I have known. Not dizzy or giddy, yet euphoric and grounded deeply in a knowing in my gut that it's required 40 years to truly trust.

It is woven in awe, entirely familiar and remembered as the very food my soul yearned for, now I am blessed to taste it. It's an experience of pure joy and infinite promise, not of things or landmarks but of unhampered possibility and purpose. The kind of love only available when the striving, pushing and forcing to make and find things outside of myself to fulfil me, had ceased. It was only possible when radical self-acceptance, and compassion for the shadow within me, began to usher in.

A love impossible to fathom, accept and allow in, until a state of surrender prevails.

When you know, you just know, they say. It's a knowing that stems from the spirit, and the spirit cares not of social timelines or matters of impropriety. True love has no conditions or rules.

It is a love that transmutes into a desire beyond the physical. A desire for *more life*. We are reminded in one another's eyes of the truth of our own beauty, our own power and the limitlessness of this existence, which cries out to be fully lived, fully expressed, fully relished and loved.

Vulnerability is the arrow that opens the heart to the purest soul-to-soul connection. It breaks down barriers, creates trust and empathy. It crumbles walls and creates the kind of honest connection that might takes years to be built through the typical ego-led interaction, which is more often our norm as humans in the world. It still makes me smile to think of just how many people remarked, 'You write so honestly in your book!', taken aback that I opted to allow myself to be truly seen.

I wrote these words just two weeks into knowing this man. It came through me fully intended for inclusion in the book. I phoned and read it to him. I asked his permission to allow me to publicly express my joy at our having been gifted to one another. We'd allowed each other in to witness our most intimate feelings in all their vulnerable glory and I let him know I wanted to share it with the world and he agreed without hesitation. Fearless.

This was all less than a fortnight after meeting him. Then there was no shadow of a doubt that it was anything but a beautiful and honest expression for the highest good. My heart was fully in the driving seat, and when love takes the reigns, fear dissolves in its wake. As I neared the deadline for submitting these chapters to my publisher Hay House, my head kicked back in and the prospect of putting myself and my new love 'out there' so very early into our union seemed ludicrous. What if it failed? *How embarrassing to have made such assured declarations*, the thought stung my ego! And I felt afraid of the potential for judgement. And so more prayer and that ever-present question: *Jessica are you being Love?* Love, who is big and mountainous and open and courageous. Love, who fears none at all for as long as she is being true – nowt can be taken from her. Love, who has won the moment she is allowed to *be*, irrespective of time, space, gender, geography or any other box we were taught to encase it in. Love, who has her own ebb and will topple all notions of *should* if she is allowed to just flow, untainted by the stain of fear.

And so here we are... Still just weeks in, I am emboldened by the declaration of our love, of my stand in being it. For there is nothing to fear. I believe that every person who enters our life comes bearing a gift, the gift of true sight. It is through our interactions with them, be it for a minute, a lifetime or several, that we are availed the opportunity to truly see ourselves. The question is always whether we are ready and willing to see.

I need not know what tomorrow holds in order to celebrate and honour today. Just imagine what might emerge from a lifetime of moments if they are each met with the fullness of the presence they deserve. We can release the grip of our clenched fists around the outcomes of our lives and instead allow...

When nothing is asked of one, a space exists for everything to be given. Sensuality is just the other side of creativity, and one begets the other. We often deny ourselves joy by waiting for it to begin.

In the space in between relationships, countries, routines and assumed identities – I discovered the invitation that the pause between cycles always presents. The invitation to know truth. The truth that to love, untainted by the desire to possess or control, is to come face to face with God.

In the sweetness of God's embrace we can know ourselves as not separate entities at all, but remember, and know ourselves, as one.

In the end, our ultimate purpose is simply that – to return to love. And from there, to know and find all of the universe, and our entire reason for being, contained in its cradle.

Our purpose has nothing at all to do with what we do. It has nothing to do with *doing* at all. On the contrary, it is a state of *being* our most authentic, realest Self. We cannot know what we are here to do before we come to discover who we truly are. As we morph into that reunion, our existence finding a new state of flow from that space of reconnection, we cannot help but find ourselves gifted with sparks of inspiration and creativity that will guide our doing. Not from a desire or need for anything outside of ourselves, but from a desire to create, birthed from a place of love, which will always nourish. As we feel the bliss that being who we truly are blesses us with, the gifts will extend far beyond our own existence, flowing out from us and into the lives of every single living being and entity.

The purpose-driven life is one that heals and uplifts humanity, unlocking potential and liberating the light inside of everyone and everything it encounters. It is always this way. And the feeling is tangible. We wake knowing we are a part of something greater than our ego's tiny and narrow desire to win, dominate or prosper. We find ourselves inspired to create meaningful things... but before we do we must *become*.

The purposeful life has recognized itself in the eyes of every other life form and knows that it cannot thrive while its brother and sister suffer. Living our purpose requires that we do not reject, resist or apologize for our joy and peace – for to do so would be to reject and resist the truth that we were made in God's own image and are here to create and be magnificent. Purpose invites us to be that joy and peace. It acts as love and that love guides our choices and actions with pure intention, and in doing so it heals the world.

Purpose asks not that our actions are lofty and sensational – though greatness is often the output of a purpose-driven soul. It asks that we find a state of presence and devote love to even the seemingly mundane or thankless tasks: washing the dishes, sweeping the street, cooking a meal. It's not about what we do, it's the intention and energy that infuses what we do that make the seemingly mundane, magical and leads us to be inspired and moved by our very own lives.

It strikes me often that to live any other way is a tragedy. I say that not through the eyes of judgement but as somebody who has known life the other way. The way of feeling stapled to a treadmill with no arrival point, always behind, lacking, never accruing enough to satiate the hole inside, locked off from the joy that is the promise and gift of true self-expression and service.

We must seek out congruence as though our lives depend on it. Indeed they do. It promises an end to the compartmentalization that robs us of our freedom and to internal conflict. It's where our intersections and polarities meet in sweet balance. Where we quit hiding and diluting and playing small and shape-shifting. Where the is-ness of who we are blazes in all its glory, and every blemish and bruise is beautiful.

We've been taught that who we are isn't enough just as is, that we have to do or become something in order to be worthy of love, when in fact we needn't do a thing, as we were *always* love. The *doing*, more often than not, simply distracts from our worth, which nestles so much deeper beneath our surface. Our work is to mine for our gold, to excavate back to our greatness, dust off the layers of all that we are not and then marvel at what lies beneath. As we become love, we draw all of life's magic unto us with divine magnetism.

To live our purpose is to be humbled and reminded of our own splendour, in equal measure. And the gilded gateway to purpose... is presence. We must seek out presence and connection as though our lives depend on it. Indeed, they do. They are the soil of intention and where we return to and choose, over and over again, who we want to be in, and for, the world.

Committing to just *be* for moments or minutes every single day, over and over throughout the day, checking in to ask ourselves *How am I feeling and what do I need?*, can catapult us back home into ourselves and to the state of awareness from which intention can reign. *Am I being love?* I ask myself, being it to myself first and then to all else. And if not, I can return, silently comforting myself: *It's OK, you just forgot who you are*, over and over, so that I can leave the legacy that for me feels most real.

Life as the Lotus

'When past pain would have you close... open.
When fear nudges you into contraction lest you
might find yourself disappointed or hurt... open.
And when the potential of failing prompts you
into shrinking... open some more.
Perhaps the bravest thing we can do in pursuit
of a life truly lived – unfurled to the abundance
that is the unfailing promise of a heart wide
open – is to allow in, and accept, all that we are
worthy of.
Know that we were created as a reflection
of God's glory and that joy, abundance and
unconditional love without limits is ours to
behold, a mirror image of who we are.
So when fear would have our petals turn
inwards in defeat and defence – a contrary
attempt to protect us from our own becoming
– the invitation is to open like the lotus flower
that we are.
Our roots are enmeshed with the earth and we
are touched and lit by the sun.
The fear is just an illusion and our job
is simply to be the beauty that we are,
in full faith that, cometh what may, in
full acceptance and knowing, I am.'

JESSICA HUIE

The irony of life, I have found, is that, between the two pillars of our existence that are fear and love, the moment we find ourselves gifted with blessings in whatever form they might take – a business or career that is flowing and feels fully aligned with all that's important to us, a relationship that nourishes and nurtures at a soul level – it isn't long before our ego, in a misguided attempt to keep us safe and protect us from perceived failure or loss, begins to wreak havoc with our joy.

Fear kicks in. Concern about what might go wrong infiltrates. Do we really have what it takes to be the boss that is required to drive the business to the destination of our devising? To be that person that our loved one sees and feels so clearly? To make a success of that thing – whatever the *thing* is – and not sabotage it? Beneath it all, the question is always whether we feel we are deserving and worthy of it. For me, the temptation is to run for cover, particularly in matters of love, where the nurture and stability is so foreign and removed from my early childhood experiences. I want to protect myself, to flee to safer, more well-trodden shores where the terrain is familiar and the ground steady, if devoid of the bliss the ocean would have me swim in – the bliss that life so wants to have me experience and recognize myself as.

It's four months since I nestled underneath a tree and let the poetry of my heart tell the story of my falling-in-love. I'm on the right side of the bed, curled up on the edge with my own arms wrapped around me. The same self-embrace I developed unconsciously when I was too young to remember. Periodically it kicks back in.

He is on the left side of the bed, seemingly sleeping easily.

The thought of leaving the cocoon of the bed is unappealing, daunting even. Today I am due to hit 'send' on these chapters to my patient editor Lucy at Hay House and I am almost paralyzed by internal conflict.

The words I shared, a pure and honest expression of the love I found, don't reflect the crater now between us in the bed. A crater illustrative of the weeks of erosion caused by fear slowly yet consistently chipping away at a love that in the early weeks felt impenetrable. We are still in love, but the vulnerability brought on by the universe delivering me everything I could have wished for in a union has invited many of my buried fears out to play, and they've been flooring me.

I feel as though I'm in a boxing ring with a heavyweight fear and even the lightest punches are knocking me to my knees with blows that come from nowhere. Just when I get back on my feet to buoy myself in a stand for love, I'm sucker-punched again.

And I want to run. How I want to run anywhere that I can bolt the door behind me and nestle back into a mode of life that doesn't come with the potential for abandonment. The conflict is that I'm on a deadline and I cannot submit the section on my love story as it is knowing full well that, as real as every letter on the page was, it is only half the story. Only part of the truth. A truth that, however much I would have liked it to be finite, stamped with a 'happily ever after' and wrapped in a silken bow, is not. Because I am not a novelist who can simply plottwist and conjure dragons and heroines to steer my story to a destination of my comfortable devising, I feel paralyzed.

All I can write is my whole truth. Not to be some misguided martyr or sacrifice my personal boundaries in the name of art, but because I have experienced first-hand the power and ripple effect that comes from casting light into the darkest corners. It heals and purifies and somehow returns us. That's the writing I need to share, simultaneously liberating myself from my own misguided shame.

There are my ego's feelings of failure in admitting that fear has been the reigning champion in my beautiful relationship of late. Then there are all the 'shoulds' that my internal critic now seizes the moment to test me with. After all, aren't I supposed to have it all worked out, Hay House author that I am? Shouldn't a mentor who supports others with living their purpose be grounded enough in her own divinity that she eats these old default fears for breakfast?

He wakes and I sit sobbing to my love and having the realest conversation I recall in a relationship yet. It is a dialogue in which he invites me to take his hand, lets me know he will walk with me on the path of continually leaning into the fear as it arises and choosing to see through the eyes of love, over and over, until thoughts of gratitude will one day replace the preempting of a danger that no longer exists. Then he reminds me that, while it is true that the untainted love we first met in has evolved, with the will to take full responsibility for our own growth and healing we can and will arrive at a place of even greater beauty and depth.

As I listen, sitting on the bathroom floor, the indomitable and powerful woman replaced by my internal, frightened little girl, I realize that this, too, is real love – not being enamoured with an *idea* of a person, but a wholesome appreciation and acceptance of their entire being. And that here again is the gift – God's invitation to realize herself.

I've never felt so undressed, sitting on those cold tiles. However my ego would have liked my love to perceive me – smart, kind, attractive, successful, confident and sexy – it was washed away by that morning's interaction in which he met all of me. Met all of me and loved me still with all of my scars, those healed and those still in need of tender nursing, now visible in the light.

And just by being who he was, I became more me than I have ever been.

I felt the magnitude of the invitation that life was presenting me with… to say yes to myself fully. My default pattern of recoiling from my deepest desires, though now spotlighted by my relationship, was unquestionably still alive in other areas of my life. I felt myself to be at the bottom of a steep mountain, uncertain as to whether I had enough water in my flask to make it to the top alive. Perhaps it sounds dramatic, but I know some – no, many – of you will know well the all-encompassing intensity of the grip of survival mechanisms that kept us safe, often developed before we were old enough to even speak.

The paradox of awareness is that we cannot unsee what we have seen, and if you've read this far, then you're also on the path back home to the you that's standing right up top of the mountain peak, overlooking the magnificence of the valleys with the clarity and purity of your bird's-eye view. When we're on this path, though we might stumble and sometimes fall, bruising ourselves and others in the process, there is only one direction we can go. Round and round we will saunter while life presents us with the very circumstances, people, challenges and possibilities to facilitate our ascendance into a deeper level of our own becoming.

We can turn and run away or hide behind pseudo-emotions and stories of our own imagining. We can intellectualize and spiritually override for entire lifetimes until we eventually decide. We choose. Just as we have chosen before and can take sustenance from the smaller hills we have already climbed.

And it starts with a square look in the mirror, unclothed, allowing ourselves to be fully seen. It's no coincidence that I spent a career helping others to become visible to the world and was very skilled and successful at it. What a sense of humour life has: it now dawns on us that all along the job is not in revealing ourselves to others, but first to let our armour and costumes fall away so we might truly see our perfectly imperfect selves, then love that reflection. Not the optics, but the rounded truth of our being – irrespective of whether that displeases the world.

There is no timeline to adhere to. Healing is an ongoing process with deeper and deeper levels of revelation. More and more sweet life is gifted to us as we dance within the full spectrum of both beholding and feeling our darkness and expanding into the fullest expression and appreciation of our light.

I can't lie. As I write this, I flit between a peaceful, serene sense of the importance of this personal sharing and a questioning of my sanity in baring my soul. The truth beneath the chatter, however, is that our healing is always our calling.

And so we must choose. Over and over again, in every minute of every day, we can cultivate the awareness that allows us to remember that each moment presents us with a choice: to choose love over fear. With each choice in the stand for love, our thoughts, words and actions become the building blocks of a life that over time cannot help but be big and courageous, joyous and abundant. We will attract more of that which we expend, for science itself now concurs that we attract what we are. Fear is self-determining, but love will set us free.

Of course, it's far from easy. As I sit here and write this, the words meet the page and are a balm and reminder for my own soul. 'No tears in the writer, no tears in the readers' says the old adage. I do cry quiet tears because allowing the blessings and the deluge of love I find life delivering to me at this time is almost as hard to be with as the challenge pain brings.

Yes, being with our blessings can be terrifying, like standing at the precipice of everything your heart desires and knowing that you only need to take a step and then be still. But, if you step, there is the possibility you might fall, and that prospect, given the memories of the bruises you've nursed from past topples and hurts, can render you near-frozen in trepidation. The child within you wants to cling desperately to whatever feels solid and sturdy and able to hold all of your weight, and your mind says you are not sure you could bare to fall down again; you don't know that you could heal again.

The quiet truth whispers softly, if we just rock our understandably angsty mind with the tenderness we'd afford a baby. Truth whispers that the healing comes from taking that step into the unpromised. That is where reclamation and reunion of and with our true self awaits. The bruised and scathed skin falls away to reveal just how golden we really are beneath our wounded and worn suits of armour. Beautiful in our vulnerability. Unstoppable in the sheer power of our fearlessness. We are not just a person, but a culmination of moonbeams and ocean drops and every atom and ion that was, is and will ever be. We are the product and legacy of all who came before us and the seed for all who will follow. We are not some lone, separate entity living in isolation of the whole; we are the very whole itself. When we open and step forward in love, we will feel this... and life will reveal all of its secrets.

As we come to know better, we get to choose new tools for the new reality we now see available to us through our evolved lens. This is where we must soften and put down the armour. Our weapons are no longer required on this plane. We can send love and compassion to the hardened places that may always live within us, grateful for their role in helping us to sift through the trenches. Reject nothing. Love ourselves even more ardently, but remember that as we step onwards and upwards our heart must lead. Then that force that was defensive, imagining the potential for trouble, failure and pain waiting around the corner, gets to be transposed into light.

Light and faith. The hardness replaced with a new steeliness that is grounded in spirit. We don't have to be brave alone. Where our minds become weak and situations arise that leave us scared and prompted into the default habits that would have us stuck, we can surrender and hand it over. We can look to the sky and ask that our faith be renewed. We can close our eyes and ask that we feel the presence of our guides. We can turn inwards and remember... remember that we are not alone. We have never been alone and we need not walk this life alone. We only need ask and it will always be given.

The combination of surrendering that which feels beyond our capacity to change whilst taking full responsibility for our growth is a potent one.

We must make becoming the highest version of ourselves our priority – and simultaneously accept and love who and where we are today.

We must do the work. There is no self-help book, meditation or magic spell that will release us from the necessity of actually sitting with the uncomfortable feelings and fears as they arise and choosing a response rather than being activated into our default reactions. This is truly the spiritual practice.

So get present with yourself morning, noon and night and use the tools of your choice – journaling, affirmations, meditations, whatever is most supportive – to reconnect to that vision of who you want to be for yourself and for this world, irrespective of what happens externally, and commit to it.

We then create new reference points for our minds and begin to find we have a new palette of thoughts from which we can co-create our lives. Our thoughts, inspiring words and actions will align with our highest vision. Becoming the love that we are – the most sacred purpose we could embark on – for all of the projects, success and dreams of impact we hold for our lives becomes available to us from that vibration.

And so my prayer, over and over and forever more, is that my love be greater than my fear. My most encompassing request is to let love lead, with faith as my anchor. In doing so, separation with all of creation dissolves, and the entire universe becomes ours to behold.

And our own liberation liberates and lights up the world.

And every step, however small, if taken in love, is one of pure and holy purpose.

Dear Reader,

Thank you for reading *Purpose*. Both writing and then sharing it with the world continues to be a gift that blesses my life.

I hope that it sparks something inside and encourages you to continue on your own journey to the fullest expression of your truth .

This is my first book and as a new author, I'd love to hear what resonated – all feedback is truly welcome! You can connect with me on Instagram @Jessica_Huie_ and visit me at my website www.JessicaHuie.com

Finally, I have a favour to ask. If you've enjoyed *Purpose*, feel inclined and can spare a few minutes, it would be great if you could place a review on the retailer's site. Every review counts and I would truly appreciate it.

One love, Jessica

ABOUT THE AUTHOR

Sydney Watson

Jessica Huie MBE is an award-winning entrepreneur and the founder of Color blind cards and JHPR - an agency representing inspiring entrepreneurs and personalities.

Today Jessica runs The Purpose Retreats and The Purpose Academy, a programme for purpose-driven small business owners ready to embrace their calling and amplify their impact in the world.

Color blind cards was the UK's first independent multicultural greetings card brand to be stocked on the British high street, and is credited with starting an early conversation around diversity in both retail and branding.

Jessica enjoys an international public-speaking career and sits on *Glamour* magazine's Power List as one of the UK's most influential women. Committed to increasing social mobility and equality, Jessica sits on the boards of several national charities and is one of Britain's 'Most Inspiring Entrepreneurs' according to the *Evening Standard* Awards. In 2014, aged just 34, she was awarded an MBE in recognition of her services to entrepreneurship and contribution to diversity.

www.JessicaHuie.com

Listen. Learn. Transform.

Reach your fullest potential with unlimited Hay House audios!

Gain access to endless wisdom, inspiration, and encouragement from world-renowned authors and teachers—guiding and uplifting you as you go about your day. With the *Hay House Unlimited* Audio app, you can learn and grow in a way that fits your lifestyle . . . and your daily schedule.

With your membership, you can:

- Let go of old patterns, step into your purpose, live a more balanced life, and feel excited again.

- Explore thousands of audiobooks, meditations, immersive learning programs, podcasts, and more.

- Access exclusive audios you won't find anywhere else.

- Experience completely unlimited listening. No credits. No limits. No kidding.

Try for FREE!

Visit **hayhouse.com/listen-free** to start your free trial and get one step closer to living your best life.

HAY HOUSE

Look within

Join the conversation about latest products,
events, exclusive offers and more.

   Hay House

   @HayHouseUK

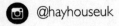   @hayhouseuk

We'd love to hear from you!